REAL MEN DO IT OUTDOORS
... AROUND THE WORLD

REAL MEN DO IT OUTDOORS
... AROUND THE WORLD

Joshua Barnes

LONGUEVILLE
BOOKS

CONTENTS

INTRODUCTION

Since the release of my last book, **Real Men Do It Outdoors: The Blokes' BBQ Cookbook**, I have embarked on a mission of barbecuing self-discovery. Leaving behind my beloved backyard barbecues, I have travelled the world in search of the best barbecue locations and cuisines as well as the most innovative and time-tested cooking techniques real men worldwide have to offer. Yes, it's a hard life, but someone has to do it!

Along my smoke filled journeys to some of the most amazing and culturally flavoursome countries in the world, I have met wonderful people, learnt a lot about barbecuing as well as myself and have been most surprised by how much my view of barbecuing has changed – I believe for the better.

Surprisingly it's not just the well known barbecue nations that have provided the greatest insights. It's also the places you may not yet have thought of. Each of these destinations has offered me a unique perspective on barbecuing, along with their distinctive flavours and styles, often shaped by local cultures, climates and the barbecuing heritage in each area.

Despite all these differences, there is one thing that remained constant. No matter where I was in the world, the welcoming and community feel at each barbecue remained the same. The humble barbecue has the ability to bring people together, no matter their age, sex, background or nationality. Its language is universal – if only I could say the same about my broken foreign language skills.

IN REAL MEN DO IT OUTDOORS — AROUND THE WORLD YOU'LL FIND:
- 'must visit' guides to the world's best barbecue destinations
- regionally-themed recipes
- personal and often humorous stories about my worldwide barbecuing adventures
- insights into the world's leading barbecue nations

WORLD TRENDS & BBQ EVOLUTION

THE FAMILY FAVOURITE

STYLISH OUTDOOR KITCHEN

A VALUABLE GIFT FROM MY recent travels has been the real life lesson in barbecuing I have gained along the way. This is the type of lesson I not only got to see, but smell, taste and consume.

Many of the countries I visited appeared untouched by time, with fresh fish and seafood barbecued on the edge of the beach in leaves, pits or hot coals, an approach perfectly suited to their relaxed beach setting.

New home builders and renovators are re-designing backyards around purpose-built barbecue areas capable of catering for a few friends or entire street parties. These stylish new areas boast comfortable lounge-style seating, outdoor heating and all the modern accessories you would expect to find in most modern kitchens, from food preparation benches, accessory drawers, to bar fridges, and they're even throwing in the kitchen sink.

However, it is not only the barbecues themselves that are changing, but also the way they're being used. More adventurous restaurant-style recipes are surfacing, influenced by a range of international flavours and

new cooking techniques, and popular cooking shows and books by celebrity chefs have led to us refusing to settle for mundane food.

The exciting part is, with all this change, the barbecue remains true to its heritage. Simple steaks and sausages cooked till black still pass as suitable barbecue fare – as long as it's accompanied by cold beer, close friends and it's all enjoyed outdoors of course!

VERSATILITY AT ITS BEST

EASY ENTERTAINER

THE RECIPES

BEER RATING

A BIG THANK YOU GOES OUT TO ALL the real men around the world who have welcomed me into their backyards and have inspired the following recipes.

These recipes are personal adaptations of local favourites discovered throughout my travels. Where necessary, some local ingredients have been modified to allow greater accessibility in a wider range of countries – without compromising flavour.

You'll see at the top of each recipe page that we've provided a Beer Rating. This relates to the overall ease of the recipe, with 1 being dead simple and 3 being a little more involved. The rating is a rough guide; however, the cooking and preparation times given are quite accurate.

MEASURES FOR SUCCESS

You may find that cooking times vary depending on your barbecue and the weather conditions – for example, if it's really windy you may find your barbecue heat fluctuates. For testing the recipes we used 20 ml (four teaspoons) tablespoon measures; however, if you don't have one of these, the average dessert spoon is just a bit smaller than this, so use one of these and adjust as necessary. Cup measures are standard cup measures (250 ml), not just any old coffee cup or tea cup you find in your cupboard! But, except for the baking recipes, being a bit out here and there really isn't going to make such a difference to the recipes.

You will soon have all the necessary knowledge required to create your own authentic international barbecue experience, be it Australian, American or Argentinean.

AUSTRALIA & NEW ZEALAND

LEADING BARBECUE NATIONS such as Australia and New Zealand continue to push the boundaries to make household kitchens obsolete, as outdoor cooking becomes a year-round event.

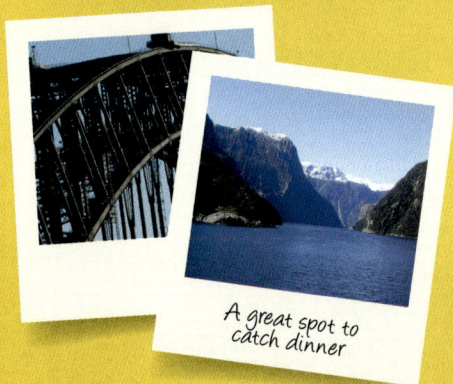

A great spot to catch dinner

TOP TIP
To peel the prawns, first pull off the head by giving it a firm tug. Then, leaving the tail on, peel off the shell and legs – they should come off quite easily. Using a sharp knife, make a shallow slit down the back and pull out the intestinal vein that runs down to the tail. Rinse under cold water and pat dry.

PRAWNS WITH COCONUT AND LIME MAYO

HEAT A FRYING PAN OVER MEDIUM heat. Add the coconut and dry-fry (ie with no oil) for 1-2 minutes, stirring regularly until golden brown. Remove from the heat immediately and transfer to a bowl to cool. Once cool, stir into the mayonnaise with 2 teaspoons of lime juice.

Peel the prawns as described on page 16. Preheat your barbecue to high. Put the prawns on the barbie in a single layer and cook for about 3 minutes, turning once, until cooked through – do not overcook. Squeeze some lime juice over the prawns then serve immediately accompanied by the coconut mayo for dipping.

PREP: 30 minutes (mostly peeling the prawns)
COOK: about 5 minutes
MAKES: 4-6 servings

25g (heaped ¼ cup) desiccated coconut
180g (¾ cup) good quality egg mayonnaise
1 lime, quartered
24 raw medium king prawns

SYDNEY ROCK OYSTERS

PUTTING UNSHUCKED OYSTERS ON the barbie for a couple of minutes helps to open them. However, you will still need an oyster shucker to complete the job properly. If you prefer not to do this, buy ready-shucked oysters on the shell.

PREP: 15 minutes (longer if using unshucked oysters)
COOK: 2-3 minutes
SERVES: 6

18-24 Sydney Rock Oysters, shucked or unshucked (if serving more people allow 3-4 each)

THAI DRESSING:
1 ½ tablespoons lime juice
1 tablespoon fish sauce
Pinch of sugar
2 small red chillies, seeded and finely chopped
1 small shallot (eschallots), finely chopped
4 kaffir lime leaves, finely chopped
1 tablespoon finely chopped coriander leaves

SIMPLE DRESSING:
About 125ml (½ cup) good quality sparkling white wine or champagne!

To make the Thai dressing, combine all the ingredients in a small jug or bowl. Set aside.

If using sparkling wine, just before serving the oysters, pour about 125ml into a jug.

If using unshucked oysters, heat your barbecue to hot. Arrange the oysters in a single layer on the barbecue and cook for about 2 minutes or until they pop open (this won't be a dramatic opening, more an unsealing of the shells), don't overcook the oysters. Remove immediately and carefully remove the top shell with an oyster shucker or blunt knife. Carefully detach each oyster from the shell, being careful not to loose much of the juices, leave in the shell. Arrange on a serving platter and either spoon a little dressing onto each one or serve a dressing or two separately.

If using shucked oysters, arrange them in their shells on a serving platter and either pour a little dressing onto each oyster before serving or serve the dressing on the side.

AUSSIE SAUSAGE SANGER WITH CHILLI AND ONION RELISH

YOU NEED A FLAT PLATE TO COOK the relish. If you don't have one make it in a frying pan beforehand. The relish can be made a day or 2 in advance, stir in the parsley just before serving. The relish can be served warm or cold.

Preheat your barbecue flat plate and grill plate to medium-high. Toss the onions in the oil then spread out on the flat plate and cook, stirring regularly for about 10 minutes. Add the chillies and cook for another minute or two. Move the onions into a pile and add the vinegar and sugar. Mix well and cook for a few more minutes. Transfer to a bowl.

Put the sausages on the grill and cook for about 10-15 minutes, turning them regularly. The cooking time will depend not only on your barbecue, but also on how thick you sausages are. Make sure they are cooked through before serving.

Serve in buttered bread rolls with plenty of relish.

PREP: 20 minutes
COOK: 30-35 minutes
SERVES: 4-8

8 good quality thick sausages
8 soft or crusty long rolls or slices of baguette, buttered

Chilli and onion relish:
2 large onions, halved and thinly sliced
3 tablespoons olive oil
2 small red chillies, finely chopped
1½ tablespoons red or white wine vinegar
3 teaspoons sugar
2 tablespoons chopped flat leaf parsley

Australia's famous barbecue spot

Wallaby ... we won't cook this one!

TOP TIP

This relish is also delicious with steak. Use either rump, sirloin or fillet steaks. If you're using thinish steaks of about 150g each, cook them on a very hot chargrill plate for about 1-1½ minutes on each side for rare and an extra minute on each side for well done.

BARBECUING DOWN UNDER

AUSTRALIANS (AUSSIES) HAVE grown up with barbecues (barbies) shaping their social calendar and providing the perfect excuse to get outdoors and enjoy one of the many stunning barbecue backdrops the country has to offer. There are blue oceans, golden surf beaches, green rainforests, white snow fields, red deserts and clear skies, spread across a large country with a relatively small population (22 million people), so you don't need to look far to find a great spot.

Barbies are an extremely informal affair, occurring almost all year round; however, they soar during summer holidays when the days are longer and there's cricket and other sport on TV.

At an Aussie barbie you can expect to see the backyard scattered with eskies and a buzz of sport from TV. Blokes are generally huddled around the backyard barbecue, beer in hand, attempting to look busy whilst telling jokes and avoiding any real work. Their girlfriends or wives are generally split between the house and the semi-outdoor living areas, almost intentionally avoiding the smoke, heat, oil, testosterone and tall stories that surround the barbecue.

In Australia, the barbecues are predominantly gas and often equipped with cooking hoods, as roasting by indirect heat is big on the Australian cooking agenda. There is a smaller percentage of Aussies who own charcoal barbecues which results in endless rivalry and debates between the gas vs charcoal cooking advocates.

If you get the chance to visit Australia, a great time is January 26, the Australia Day holiday, which is without a doubt the biggest barbie day of the year. People flock to friends' backyards and public barbecue areas to celebrate the day. Bring along a six pack of your favourite beer and you'll soon feel truly Australian!

GREAT REEF!

Having hired a yacht to sail the Whitsunday Islands, a few friends and I were ready for a holiday of fishing, barbecuing and relaxing, with a few quiet beers on the side.

After a few hours of unsuccessful fishing, our once grand plans of freshly caught barbecued fish dinners were looking more and more grim. As we reeled in our lines for the evening, ready to admit defeat, we heard a loud thump. Had we run aground? Then again, thump, thump, thump.

As we looked towards the bow of the boat, we saw squid jumping straight out of the water into the bright lights of the boat and to our delight – onto our deck. We all enjoyed barbecued calamari and every possible variation of cooked calamari you can imagine across the next couple of days – what more could you ask for?!

KIWI LAMB CUTLETS WITH GRILLED VEGETABLES

LEAVING THE CUTLETS TO MARINATE for a bit before cooking would be good, but the grilled vegetables have plenty of flavour as well, so it isn't vital.

Marinate the cutlets while you get the vegetables ready. Trim the cutlets of any excess fat. Combine 2 table-spoons of the oil with the garlic and some black pepper. Pour this over the cutlets rubbing it into the meat with your hands. Cover and marinate for 30 minutes or up to 4 hours, put them in the fridge if marinating for longer than 30 minutes.

Slice the zucchini lengthways into slices about 2mm thick. Slice the capsicum into strips about 3cm wide, removing any seeds and membrane. Slice the potato into 2mm thick slices. Put them all in a large bowl and add the remaining 2 tablespoons of oil and plenty of salt and pepper. Mix well to coat everything. You may need to do this in two batches.

Take the meat out of the fridge to come to room temperature. Pre-heat the hot plates and grill on your barbecue to high. Put the potatoes on the hot plates and cook for 3 minutes. Brush with oil then turn over. Remove them as they are cooked through. Meanwhile, put the zucchini and capsicum onto the grill and cook for 2 minutes on each side, until they are soft and have good stripes on them.

Arrange on a serving plate with the potatoes. Scatter over the olives and parsley and drizzle with a little extra oil if liked.

Put the lamb cutlets on the chargrill and cook for 1-2 minutes on each side for rare or a little longer if you prefer your meat more cooked. Serve accompanied by the vegetables.

PREP: 30 minutes
COOK: 8-10 minutes
SERVES: 4

Allow 3-4 lamb cutlets per person, depending on the size
4 tablespoons olive oil
3 big garlic cloves, crushed
Salt and freshly ground black pepper

VEGETABLES:
2 medium zucchini
1 red capsicum
600g (about 3 large) potatoes
100g pitted kalamata olives, halved
2 tablespoons roughly chopped flat leaf parsley, optional

RED WINE AND HERB ROASTED AUSSIE BEEF

COMBINE THE RED WINE, ROSEMARY and olive oil and season with black pepper (not salt at this point). Count your slices of garlic, then using the point of a sharp knife, make the same number of small, deep slits all over the beef. Push a garlic slice into each one. If you have a ziplock bag, put the beef into it and pour in the marinade. Seal the bag, then turn the meat several times to evenly coat it. Put into a bowl and leave to marinate in the fridge for at least 4 hours. If you don't have a ziplock bag, put the beef in a dish, pour over the marinade, turn a few times then refrigerate. Either way, turn the beef every 30 minutes to ensure it is evenly coated. Remove from the fridge 20-30 minutes before cooking to allow it to return to room temperature. Remove the beef from the marinade and pat dry, reserve the marinade.

Ideally you want indirect heat for cooking the beef so it doesn't just blacken on the outside. If using a gas barbie, heat all the burners to medium then sit the beef in the middle, or where you are able to turn off the heat below. Turn off the heat below the beef, leaving the other burners on. Close the hood and cook for about 50 minutes for juicy and rare meat, for another 10 minutes for medium or until it is cooked to your liking. Turn the meat and baste with the reserved marinade every 10 minutes, to prevent it burning

on the outside. The exact cooking time will depend on the thickness of your beef and your barbecue. Remember the beef will continue to cook while it is resting.

If using a charcoal barbecue (you must have a hood), heat the coals for about 45 minutes then put a baking tray on top of the coals, but underneath the grill rack. Cook as above.

Brush the mushrooms with olive oil and season well with salt and black pepper. Set aside.

Once the beef is cooked, remove from the barbecue, season with sea salt and rest covered with foil for about 10 minutes. While it is resting cook the mushrooms for about 5 minutes turning once, until soft.

Serve the beef in thick slices accompanied by the chargrilled mushrooms.

PREP: 15 minutes, plus at least 4 hours marinating time
COOK: (about) 55 minutes
SERVES: 8 (see box for other quantities)

250ml (1 cup) decent red wine
1 rosemary sprig, leaves only
1 tablespoon olive oil
Sea salt and black pepper
2 garlic cloves, thinly sliced
1.5kg piece eye fillet, tied (ask your butcher to do this)
8 large field mushrooms

SMALLER QUANTITIES
If you want to serve this for fewer people, you'll need about 1.2kg for 6 people and just under 1kg for 4. Keep the marinade ingredients the same, but reduce the number of mushrooms, allowing 1 per person. Cook the beef for slightly less time.

Hmm ... prime for the barbie

HOW TO ROAST THE AUSTRALIAN WAY

ROASTING IN A COVERED BARBECUE is very similar to roasting in a wall oven, with the benefits of added flavour and being outdoors, taking heat out of the kitchen during summer.

If you have one, it's recommended you remove the solid plate, leaving only the grill. This allows better heat flow under the hood. Move the grill to the centre, creating a platform on which you can place your roast holder or baking dish. If you don't have these items, simply place the food on the grill.

Start by heating your barbecue to the desired temperature (medium-hot). Most hoods will have a temperature gauge on the front; if not, you can buy them at all good barbecue stores.

Once at the required temperature, turn off the centre burners under where the food will sit, or move the coals to the side, so it cooks by indirect heat.

Add the roast holder, meat and drip pan before closing the hood.

Try not to open the hood to check the meat as this will cause the temperature to fluctuate and extend the cooking time.

When it's due to be ready, use a meat thermometer to check the internal heat of the meat to confirm it is ready.

Tip: To ensure a tender, juicy roast, you may also include a small container of water (or beer) next to the roast to stop it from drying out. Alternatively, wrap it in foil midway through cooking. During the roasting process, it is also important that you enjoy cold beers.

Tip: Sear meat quickly to seal in the juice prior to roasting, or set the starting temperature slightly higher than normal prior to putting the meat in, then return to usual cooking temperature shortly afterwards.

BEST BEERS FOR A BARBIE

It's not much of a surprise to hear that Aussies don't mind a beer. In fact, they're about as crazy about beer as they are about barbecuing. People will generally turn up to barbecues in Australia with a sixpack (6 beers), or a case of beer (24 beers), depending upon how long they're planning on staying.

Expect to see an esky full of Tooheys in New South Wales, XXXX in Queensland or VB if you're in Victoria, although recently boutique beers have exploded onto the scene. This has been driven largely by Aussies demanding a greater variety of styles and flavours from their beers.

If you're heading to a barbecue in Australia, make sure you try Prime Beer – it's made specifically to complement barbecued red meat!

KANGAROO

DON'T BE SCARED OF COOKING kangaroo, just don't overcook it otherwise you could easily end up with a dry, leathery piece of meat. It's an incredibly lean meat, low in fat and cholesterol and very high in protein, so it's pretty good for you. It's best to marinate the meat before cooking, which will also help prevent it drying out while cooking.

Remove visible fat or sinew from the fillets and place in a shallow dish. Combine the olive oil and honey with plenty of black pepper. Pour over the meat, cover and leave to marinate in the fridge for at least one hour and up to four.

Meanwhile, heat a dry frying pan over high heat and dry fry the macadamia nuts until golden brown. Remove from the pan immediately and set aside to cool. Whisk together the olive oil, balsamic vinegar and add salt and black pepper.

Just before cooking the kangaroo, combine the salad leaves, avocado and tomato in a serving dish.

Remove the kangaroo from the fridge 20 minutes before cooking to allow it to come to room temperature. Remove from the marinade and pat dry with kitchen paper. Preheat barbecue to hot. Sear the fillets for 4-5 minutes on one side, turn over and cook for a further 4 minutes, or until medium-rare, do not overcook. Remove from the heat and leave to rest for a few minutes while putting the finishing touches to the salad. Whisk the dressing again to combine everything then pour over the salad and top with the basil leaves. Thinly slice the kangaroo across the grain, this is the best way to slice it to keep it tender and arrange on top of the salad. Season with salt, scatter over the macadamia nuts and serve.

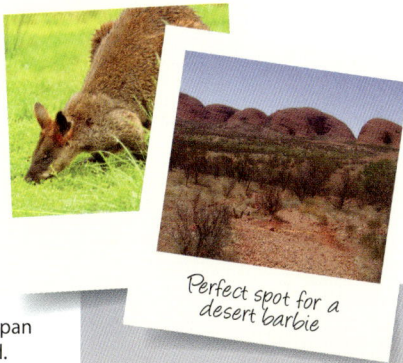

PREP: 30 minutes
COOK: 8-10 minutes
SERVES: 4

4 kangaroo fillets, 130-150g each, preferably fat rather than thin steaks
3 tablespoons (1/4 cup) olive oil
1 tablespoon honey
Freshly ground black pepper

SALAD:
40g macadamia nuts, roughly chopped
4 tablespoons (1/3 cup) olive oil
2 tablespoons white balsamic vinegar (or black if you don't have it)
Sea salt and freshly ground black pepper
100g mixed salad leaves
1 ripe avocado, chopped
250g cherry tomatoes, halved round the middle (they look prettier)
Small handful fresh basil leaves

Perfect spot for a desert barbie

GRILLED BARRAMUNDI AND FENNEL WITH A WARM PINE NUT DRESSING

SLICE OFF THE LONG TOP STALKS OF the fennel, leaving about 2cm intact. Reserve any feathery fronds you may have. Slice the fennel lengthways into slices about 1cm thick. Brush with olive oil, season with salt and pepper and set aside. Roughly chop any reserved fronds.

Wash the barramundi fillets and pat dry with paper towel. Brush with oil, season with salt and black pepper and set aside.

Heat a small saucepan over medium-high heat. Add the pine nuts and dry fry until golden, shaking the pan regularly. Remove from the heat, cool slightly then add the oil and vinegar and season with salt and pepper. Add about 1 tablespoon of chopped fennel fronds, if you have any. Set aside.

Preheat your barbecue to medium-high. Arrange the fennel in a single layer on the grill and cook for about 5 minutes on each side. After a minute or 2 add the barramundi and cook for 3- 4 minutes on each side or until cooked through. If your fennel slices are a little thicker than 1cm they may take a bit longer to cook, so maybe start plating up the rest of the food while it finishes cooking.

Very briefly warm the dressing in the saucepan, either on the barbecue or on the stove top. Divide the spinach and salad leaves between four plates, top with the barramundi and fennel then spoon a little dressing over each. Serve immediately.

PREP: 15 minutes,
COOK: about 10 minutes
SERVES: 4

1 large or 2 medium fennel bulbs
Olive oil, for brushing
4 x 150-180g barramundi fillets
50g baby spinach leaves
50g mixed salad leaves

WARM PINE NUT DRESSING:

40g pine nuts
4 tablespoons olive oil
1½ tablespoons balsamic vinegar
Salt and black pepper

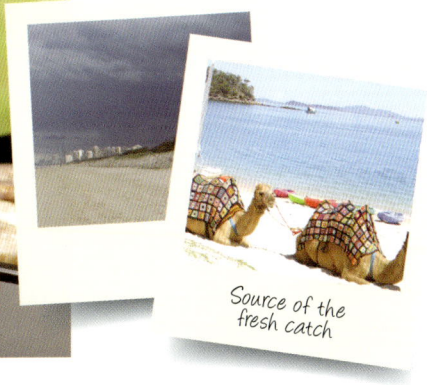

Source of the fresh catch

MORTON BAY BUGS WITH LEMON AND PARSLEY

2 BEER RATING

IF YOUR BUGS ARE ALIVE YOU NEED to make them unconscious before preparing them. The most humane way to do this is to put them in the freezer for about 45 minutes. This should be sufficient time to knock them unconscious but not long enough to freeze them completely. To prepare the bugs for cooking, place the bugs, hard shell down, on a chopping board. Then insert the tip of a sharp knife under the joint between the head and body. Pull off the head. Cut down the centre from the tail to the top. Gently split the shell open to flatten the bug. Pull out the intestinal tract, this is the black vein that runs along the back, snip off any loose pieces of shell if liked. The bug meat is now ready for cooking. Refrigerate until ready to cook.

Squeeze the juice from one lemon half and cut the remaining half into 4 long wedges. Combine the juice with the oil and parsley and season with salt and plenty of freshly ground black pepper. Brush the bugs with this flavoured oil.

Preheat barbecue grill plate to high. Add the bugs, shell side down and grill for 4-7 minutes until just cooked, (larger ones will take about 7 minutes, but smaller ones should be cooked in 4) brushing occasionally with the oil – don't over cook the bugs or you will spoil the meat. Serve immediately accompanied by lemon wedges.

These can be served on their own or accompanied by a simple green salad or for a more substantial meal accompany them with the potato salad recipe on the next page.

TOP TIP

Try and buy the freshest bugs you can. If buying green bugs that are not already cooked, ask how long ago they were alive. The best test for fresh bugs is to check that they have a fresh ocean smell. Bugs should only be stored for short periods even when chilled properly, leaving no more than 48 hours between when they are alive and when they're cooked.

PREP: 30 minutes (plus freezing the bugs)
COOK: 4-7 minutes (depending on size)
SERVES: 4

12 medium or 8 large Morton Bay Bugs (see tip box on buying Bugs)
1 lemon, halved lengthways
3 tablespoons olive oil
3 tablespoons chopped fresh flat leaf parsley
Salt and freshly ground black pepper

TASMANIAN SALMON WITH POTATO SALAD

TASMANIAN SALMON RANKS AMONG some of the best in the world. It's quick and easy to cook and it's good for you as it's low in calories and cholesterol and is a rich source of those often talked about omega-3 essential fatty acids – vital for healthy hearts and minds.

Cook the potatoes in boiling, salted water for about 8-10 minutes, until they just feel soft when pricked with a sharp knife or fork. Don't over-cook them. Put into a serving bowl. Combine the olive oil and lemon juice, season with salt and pepper and pour over the potatoes. Toss gently, then leave to cool.

Heat your barbecue to medium-high. Brush each salmon fillet with a little oil. Cook, skin-side up first (if the skin is still on) for 2-3 minutes on one side, then carefully turn over and cook for a further 2 minutes. It should still be a bit pink on the inside, otherwise the fish will be too dry. Add the capers, onion, olives and parsley to the potatoes, mix gently and serve alongside the salmon.

The fish and salad, can be served hot, warm or cold, but remember if serving the fish cold, you may want to cook it for a slightly shorter time as it will continue to cook even after it's taken off the barbie.

PREP: 15 minutes
COOK: (about) 15 minutes
SERVES: 4

750g small salad potatoes, scrubbed not peeled
4 tablespoons olive oil, plus a bit extra
1½ tablespoons lemon juice
Salt and black pepper
4 (180-200g each) Tasmanian Atlantic salmon fillets
1 tablespoon capers
½ small red onion, thinly sliced
50g small black olives
2-3 tablespoons flat leaf parsley leaves, roughly torn

Always be on the lookout for a good barbie spot

COLESLAW

NO AUSSIE BARBIE IS COMPLETE without a bowl of coleslaw. Some can be a bit heavy and tart so we've made this one a little bit lighter.

Heat a frying pan over medium-high heat throw in the hazelnuts and dry-fry for about 3 minutes until golden and toasted. Remove and leave to cool. Roughly chop when cool.

Combine the mayonnaise with the olive oil, vinegar, lemon juice, 1 tablespoon of water and mustard and season with salt and pepper.

In a separate large bowl, combine the cabbage, carrots and capers. Pour over the dressing and mix lightly. Transfer to a serving dish and scatter over the hazelnuts.

This can be made up to 4 hours in advance, top with the hazelnuts just before serving.

PREP: 20 minutes
SERVES: 4-6

30g skinned hazelnuts
4 tablespoons (1/3 cup) good quality egg mayonnaise
2 tablespoons olive oil
2 teaspoons white wine vinegar
2 teaspoons lemon juice
1 teaspoon French or wholegrain mustard
Salt and pepper
225g (about ¼) cabbage, finely shredded
300g (2) carrots, grated
2 tablespoons capers, rinsed and chopped (optional)

HOW TO COOK AUSTRALIA'S PERFECT STEAK

IF YOU OWN A BARBECUE, YOU ARE already one step closer to cooking the perfect steak. A hot barbecue grill and carefully selected steak will quickly become 'the perfect steak' if you follow this simple 10-step guide.

1 Pick the perfect steak – look for bright red colours and marbling, preferably 2.5+ cm thick, which will require enough cooking time to cara-melise on the outside and remain pink and juicy in the middle.

2 Let the steak reach room tempera-ture before grilling (15-20 minutes).

3 Get your barbecue to a high heat, ensuring it is sufficiently oiled so that the meat will not stick to the grill.

4 Crack open an icy-cold stubby of beer and enjoy the outdoors while the barbecue heats up.

5 Don't trim fat from the steak until after it has been barbecued – cooking with the fat still attached will add extra flavour to the meat.

6 Immediately prior to cooking, rub in salt and a pinch of pepper – don't add the salt any earlier as it will draw out too much moisture from the steak.

7 Place the steak on the hottest part of the grill (often directly above the burner or above the hottest coals towards the middle of the grill) and when juices appear on the top, turn it over and close the cooking hood

(if you have one), then allow to cook depending upon your tastes.

8 The 'turn only once' rule is widely accepted for cooking steaks. It sears the steak on one side, sealing in the juices. (This is a perfect world approach, not allowing for windy or cold days, so don't be afraid to use your own judgement and give the steak a second turn, for a short period).

9 If you have a roasting hood, close it after the first turn to take advan-tage of the indirect heat from within the cooking hood as well as the direct heat from the grill.

10 Allow to rest prior to serving.

MIXED BERRY PAVLOVA

A FAVOURITE DESSERT AND amazingly this one is done on the barbecue! To make this successfully on your barbie you must have a big barbecue to ensure proper indirect heat. Any direct heat under the pavlova will destroy it. This can't really be done on a coal barbecue. This version is flatter than many others.

Draw a 22cm (9inch) circle on a piece of greaseproof or baking paper. Put the paper on a lightly greased baking tray, ink side down. Preheat barbecue to 140°C (275°F/Gas 1), lighting only the outside burners and leaving the middle section cold. Find a deep ovenproof dish.

Put the egg whites in a large, clean, dry bowl. It is very important that there is no yolk in with the whites, otherwise they won't whisk. Using electric beaters (it's hard work using a hand held beater!), beat the egg whites slowly until a frothy foam forms. Then increase the speed and whisk until soft peaks form. Add the sugar a heaped large spoonful at a time, whisking well after each addition. Continue whisking until the mixture is stiff and glossy and all the sugar has dissolved. Sift in the cornflour and gently stir in the vinegar.

Spoon the meringue onto the circle, then smooth the top and sides to fill the circle, making the edges slightly higher than the center.

Put the ovenproof dish on the barbecue as much on the cooler part as possible, then carefully sit the pavlova tray on top. Carefully close the hood and cook with the hood down for 1½ hours, ensuring the temperature stays at 140°C then turn off the barbie and leave to cool for 1 hour.

When cold, carefully remove the baking paper from the bottom and transfer to a large serving dish. Whip the cream with the icing sugar and vanilla (if using) until soft peaks form. Pile on top of the pavlova then scatter over the berries. Serve at once, otherwise the cream will start to make the meringue soggy.

IN ADVANCE
This pavlova is best made on the morning that it is to be eaten. Top with the whipped cream (which can be whipped and refrigerated in advance) and fruit just before serving.

PREP: 35 minutes
COOK: 1½ hours, plus cooling time
SERVES: 8

4 egg whites
200g caster (superfine) sugar
2 teaspoons cornflour
1 teaspoon white vinegar
300ml whipping cream
2 tablespoons icing (confectioners') sugar (optional)
1 teaspoon pure vanilla extract (optional)
600g mixed berries, such as strawberries (halved if large), blueberries and raspberries

TOP TIP
For those new to the barbie, it's equivalent to cooking in the oven at 140°C (275°F/Gas 1) for 1½ hours, then turning off the oven and leaving it to cool with the door slightly ajar – put a wooden spoon in the door to prevent it closing.

TOPPING IDEAS
Instead of using cream whisk 500g mascarpone cheese with 300g lemon curd, then top with your choice of fruit.

FRUIT IDEAS
Sliced banana and raspberry coulis. To make the coulis, push fresh or (defrosted) raspberries through a sieve. Pour over sliced banana just before serving.

Top with 600g halved and seeded black and white grapes.

Top with 600g peeled, halved lengthways and sliced kiwi fruit. Spoon passionfruit pulp over to serve.

THE UNITED STATES OF AMERICA

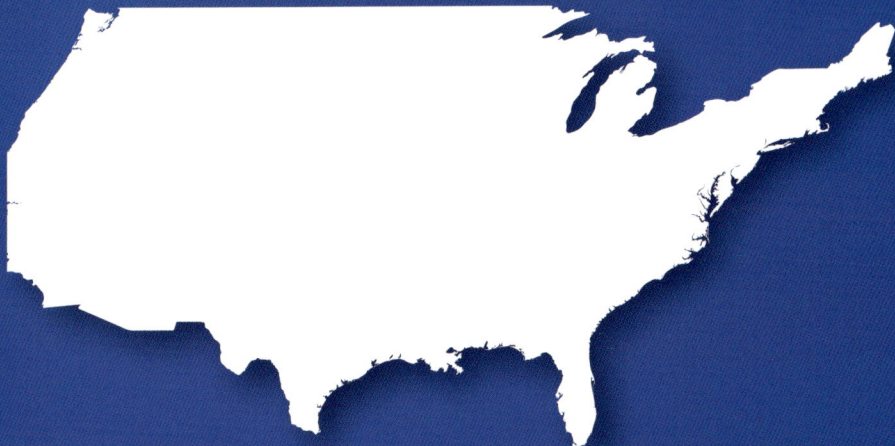

THE UNITED STATES IS LIKE
Disneyland for barbecuing enthusiasts.
It's exciting, it's fun and there's a new
adventure around every corner. And like
a big kid being dragged out of the gates
of Disneyland at closing time, I too had
to be dragged away from the US kicking
and screaming. There was still too much
barbecuing fun to be had!

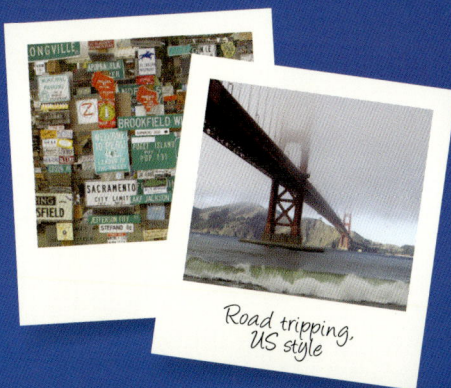

Road tripping,
US style

NEW ORLEANS CREOLE-STYLE PRAWNS/SHRIMP

1 BEER RATING

AN AUTHENTIC SHRIMP CREOLE IS hard to do on the barbie, so instead we've taken the amazing combination of herbs and spices of a traditional Creole seasoning and used them to make a great marinade. It's pretty spicy, so use less paprika and cayenne if you don't want it too spicy.

Peel and de-vein the prawns (as per recipe on p16). Wash, pat dry and put into a bowl.

Heat a dry frying pan over medium heat. Put the paprika, cayenne, black pepper, garlic powder and onion powder in the pan and dry-fry for about 1 minute stirring regularly, ensuring the spices don't burn. Remove from the heat when you get a wonderfully aromatic aroma. Immediately transfer to a small bowl and add the thyme, oregano and salt, mix well. Stir in the oil and combine.

Pour over the prawns and toss well to ensure all the prawns are coated in the oil. Set aside for 30 minutes in the fridge if you have time, but don't worry if you don't.

Cook the prawns on a hot barbecue in a single layer for about 3 minutes, turning once, until cooked through – do not overcook. Serve immediately, accompanied by wedges of lemon or lime for squeezing over.

PREP: 15-20 minutes
COOK: about 5 minutes
MAKES: 4 servings (makes 20 prawns)

20 medium king prawns
½-1 teaspoon sweet paprika
½-1 teaspoon ground cayenne pepper
1 teaspoon ground black pepper
1 teaspoon garlic powder
1 teaspoon onion powder
1 teaspoon dried thyme
1 teaspoon dried oregano
½ teaspoon of salt
3 tablespoons olive oil
1 lemon or lime, optional

You've gotta love the big green egg smoker

US underground barbecue?

JERK BUFFALO CHICKEN

THE SAME WAY BUFFALO WINGS, with their classic spicy vinegar based sauce, were too good to remain only in Buffalo NY, this Jerk chicken recipe is just too good to remain on wings alone, so we've used as many different pieces of chicken as we could find.

Put the oil in a small bowl, then whisk in the lime juice, orange juice and vinegar. Brush all over the chicken pieces and set aside.

In a separate bowl combine the remaining ingredients then use to coat the chicken all over, ensuring lots sticks to the chicken. Put into a non-metallic dish in the fridge and leave for 1-3 hours.

Remove the chicken from the fridge about 20 minutes before cooking to allow to come to room temperature. Preheat barbecue to medium. Different pieces of meat will require different cooking times. Turn the chicken fairly regularly to ensure even cooking. The skin can blacken a bit but don't let it burn too much. Ensure the chicken is cooked through before serving. Cook wings for about 20 minutes, legs and thighs for 15-20 minutes and breast for 10-12 minutes. Best eaten with your fingers, so provide lots of napkins. Serve accompanied by baked potatoes and green salad.

PREP: 30 minutes
COOK: about 20 minutes
MAKES: 4 servings

60ml (¼ cup) olive oil
1 tablespoon lime
1½ tablespoons orange juice
1½ tablespoons white wine vinegar
6 pieces of chicken - legs, thighs, wings or breast (preferably skin on)
1 Scotch Bonnet pepper (habaneros), seeded and finely chopped
1 tablespoon ground allspice
1 tablespoon dried thyme
1 teaspoon ground cinnamon
1 teaspoon paprika
1 teaspoon freshly ground black pepper
¾ teaspoon ground nutmeg
2 garlic cloves, crushed
1 tablespoon sugar
Baked potatoes and green salad, to serve

Time to spice it up

On to another barbecue ...

PORK BUTT (SHOULDER) MEMPHIS STYLE

3 BEER RATING

MUST BE COOKED ON A HOODED OR KETTLE BARBECUE

THIS IS THE TYPE OF DRY RUB mixture you'd expect to taste when visiting Rib Joints (restaurants) in Memphis, Tennessee. The dry rub along with the extended cooking time works extremely well to create tender and tasty Pork Butt (shoulder).

A barbecue thermometer is pretty vital for this recipe and a meat thermometer will also really help.

Wash and pat dry the pork shoulder and rub all over with oil. Combine the remaining ingredients and rub all over the meat to coat well, rubbing it into the meat. Set aside for at least an hour (and up to 12 hours) in the fridge and then remove from the fridge for 15 minutes to return to room temperature

Preheat your barbecue to low, about 100-120°C (215-250°F/gas ½), using an oven thermometer as a guide. If you are able to, turn off one side of the barbecue, but keeping the internal temperature as above, if not turn the heat down on one side as low as possible.

Put the pork on the turned-off/cooler side and cook for at least 5 hours, turning and rotating the meat every 30 minutes or so. It's very important to keep an eye on the temperature and adjust as necessary as this could fluctuate, particularly if it is a windy day. After about 2½ hours wrap the pork in a double layer of foil.

By the end of cooking the meat should be very, very tender and fall apart. To check that the meat is properly cooked, insert a meat thermometer into the thickest part, it should read at least 75°C (165°F), however to pull it apart you'll need to reach about 80-90°C (180-190°F). Transfer to a large plate in the foil and rest for 30 minutes to 1 hour. Pull the meat apart or slice if preferred. Try and pull-apart the pork just before serving, as it can dry out quickly. This is best served with a sauce such as the BBQ sauce on p50.

PREP: 10 minutes
COOK: about 5 hours
MAKES: 6-8 servings

1 boneless, skinless pork shoulder roast (2kg (4.5lb) will serve about 6 and 2.5kg (5.5lb) will serve about 8)
2 teaspoons vegetable oil
2 teaspoons garlic powder
2 teaspoons onion powder
2 teaspoons ground black pepper
2 teaspoons paprika
2 teaspoons cumin powder
2 teaspoons brown sugar
1 teaspoon salt
1 teaspoon chilli powder
½ teaspoon cayenne pepper
½ teaspoon mustard powder

LIVING THE U.S. DREAM

NOW THAT I'M HOME AND IT'S TIME to write this chapter about my barbecue experiences in the US, I begin with nervous anticipation. How can I possibly do this amazing barbecuing nation justice in just a few short pages, when others have spent their entire lives studying this phenomenon?

I guess I simply start by saying you need to see it with your own eyes to believe it. It makes you step back and think, 'Wow, I thought I was crazy about barbecuing, but these guys really take barbecuing to the next level'!

In a way the US is similar to other countries, with the social occasion of barbecuing being enjoyed country-wide. Real men take advantage of great weather, weekends, holidays such as the 4th of July, Memorial Day and Labor Day, and major sporting events like the football (NFL) and baseball (MLB) to get together and enjoy great food, great friends and, of course, the great outdoors.

But that's where the similarities end. The large geographic scale, various food influences and cooking styles, along with the vast range of barbecues available, sets each US region apart, not only from each other but the rest of the world.

The most interesting of which is the barbecuing heartland of the United States. This includes the cities of Memphis and Kansas City along with the entire states of North Carolina and Texas which are widely renowned for their contribution to barbecuing. Although each region offers greatly different experiences, they are all tied together by their shared passion and flair for barbecuing and were the highlights of my US travels.

At the point where I became overwhelmed by the intensity of barbecuing in the US, I discovered an even more serious side. There are barbecue groups, associations, clubs, barbecue cook-offs, and large-scale competitions between Pit Masters and barbecuing professionals that continue to push the boundaries of cooking. No matter what time of the year you travel to the US, you'll be sure to find a number of barbecue championships and events on the social calendar, celebrating barbecuing of all different types.

BEEF BRISKET WITH TEXAS-STYLE RUB

3 BEER RATING

MUST BE COOKED ON A HOODED OR KETTLE BARBECUE

AS BRISKET CONTAINS A LOT OF connective tissue and fat it requires very long, slow cooking to make it juicy and tender to eat. If you rush it you will end up with a pretty inedible piece of meat. An oven thermometer is pretty vital for this recipe and a meat thermometer will also really help.

Look over the meat and trim any excessive amounts of fat, leaving a layer about 1cm (¼ inch) thick which will help keep the meat moist during cooking, (any more could cause a fat fire on the barbie). Rinse in lukewarm water and pat dry with paper towel. Combine the rub ingredients and rub well all over the meat. Set side for 45 minutes in the fridge. Then for 15 minutes out of the fridge to return to room temperature.

Preheat your barbecue to low heat, 120-150°C (250-300°F/Gas 1-2), using an oven thermometer as a guide. If you are able to, turn off one side of the barbecue, but keeping the internal temperature as above, if not turn the heat down on one side as low as possible. Put the meat on the cooler side and cook for about 2½ hours (30 minutes per 450g (1lb) of meat), turning and rotating the meat regularly and brushing with a little beer to keep it moist. It's very important to keep an eye on the temperature and adjust as necessary as this could fluctuate, particularly if it is a windy day. After 2½ hours, brush with beer and wrap the meat in a double layer of foil and continue to cook for a further 2½ hours and until the internal temperature of the meat reaches 85°C (190°F), measured in the thickest part of the meat. Once again keep an eye on the temperature during this time.

Remove from the heat, taking care not to spill any of the juices, and still wrapped in the foil, wrap in a towel and preferably leave for a further 2 hours to relax and allow the meat to re-absorb its juices. If you can't wait this long, leave it for at least 30 minutes. Slice the meat and serve accompanied by barbecue sauce (page 50).

PREP: 10 minutes
COOK: about 5 hours, plus 2 hours resting
MAKES: 6 servings

2.5kg (5lb) piece flat-cut or point-cut beef brisket
½ bottle of beer

RUB:
2 tablespoons brown sugar
3 teaspoons paprika
1 teaspoon freshly ground black pepper
2 teaspoons garlic powder
2 teaspoons onion powder
1 teaspoon dried parsley
½ teaspoon salt
¼ teaspoon ground cumin
¼ teaspoon ground cinnamon
¼ teaspoon ground coriander
¼ teaspoon dried oregano
¼ teaspoon chilli powder

BUTCHER SHOP STEAKHOUSE

Preparing for the big day

UNO CHICAGO GRILL
Another lunch grill; why not?

LA BBQ BACON CHEESEBURGER

2 BEER RATING

PUT THE MINCE IN A BOWL AND ADD the salt and pepper, onion, garlic, tomato sauce and egg and mix well until thoroughly combined. Add sufficient fresh breadcrumbs to bind it together. Shape into 6 round patties. Cover and chill for 1-2 hours.

Preheat barbecue to medium-hot and cook the patties on each side for 4-5 minutes, or until cooked to your liking. Sit a slice of cheese on each burger for the final few minutes of cooking. Cook the bacon on the barbecue for a few minutes, until cooked to your liking. Grill the buns for 30 seconds on each side. Top each bun base with some lettuce, a cheeseburger and bacon, then top with additional toppings, if liked. Serve immediately accompanied by tomato sauce.

TOP TIP

Although you could use breadcrumbs from a box it's much better to use freshly made breadcrumbs. If possible, use day-old bread with the crusts removed and process in a food processor into fine breadcrumbs. If you don't have old bread, dry fresh bread in a hot oven for 5 minutes or so, cool then process.

PREP: 30 minutes
COOK: about 10 minutes
MAKES: 6

BURGER PATTIES:
750g beef mince (make sure it has a bit of fat in it)
Salt and freshly ground black pepper
1 small onion, finely chopped
2 garlic cloves, crushed
1 tablespoon tomato sauce (ketchup)
1 egg, lightly beaten
About 60g fresh breadcrumbs (see box)
6 slices cheddar or mozzarella cheese
8 bacon rashers, halved
6 good quality burger buns or round bread rolls, halved
Shredded lettuce
Sliced tomato

VENICE BEACH CORN!

AFTER CHECKING OUT THE HOMES of Hollywood stars, hoping I'd get invited in for a barbecue with Sly Stallone or Big Arnie, I ventured on to Venice beach for some people watching and to find some much needed food.

Upon arrival, and to my delight, something caught my eye: a street vendor selling mouth watering barbecued corn. I ordered a cob and, almost in unison with the street vendor attentively turning the corn, my head turned to watch people passing by on skates, beach cruiser bikes and everything in between, draped in uniquely Californian apparel.

In no time, my corn was cooked to perfection. A little bit of charcoal along with lots of salt and butter and it was ready to eat. Cob in hand I continued walking towards Santa Monica Pier – looking at this photo I can taste the salty barbecued corn. It's amazing what an impact a simple barbecue meal can have on your lasting memories.

Don't leave home without your barbecue

PIT MASTERS — ART OR SCIENCE?

In the US, barbecue professionals and the highly regarded Pit Masters (elite barbecuers) have many weapons in their barbecuing arsenal.

Their barbecues range from basic grills, kettles and those you'd expect to see in most backyards to upright smokers, big green eggs, converted 44 gallon drums, home-made pits and even custom-built mobile rigs that look like they've come out of the space program.

Once the barbecue has been chosen, it's down to the skill and experience of the Pit Master to turn meat into magic.

There are gas, charcoal and wood fire fuels, hot and cold smoke, various hardwoods, complex dry rubs, sauces, dips and bastes, and methods for guaranteeing moist flavoursome food such as brines, injecting and beer-can chicken. For the Pit Master it is a science and an art form, not just a social occasion.

THE BEST OF THE BEST: MEMPHIS AND ROYAL

Barbecue championships are held from coast to coast, giving barbecue enthusiasts and Pit Masters the opportunity to challenge each other and themselves to deliver world class food. Two renowned championships include Memphis in May and Royal American Barbecue.

Memphis in May is a world championship contest. Each year hundreds of teams cook up their best version of pork ribs, shoulder and whole hogs in an attempt to win over $100,000 in prize money and endless bragging rights. If the hundreds of barbecues aren't enough to convince you that these guys are crazy about barbecuing, perhaps the Ms Piggie Idol competition where real men dress up in pig outfits and sing songs about barbecue pork will change your mind!

The American Royal Barbecue, held in Kansas City, Missouri, was first run in 1980 and is the birthplace of KC Masterpiece barbecue sauce, which was awarded first place and everlasting barbecue credibility and fame! The event now has over 500 teams competing in multiple categories – no wonder it's known as the 'World Series of Barbecue'.

BARBECUED SPARE RIBS

MUST BE COOKED ON A HOODED OR KETTLE BARBECUE

IN AMERICA RIBS ARE FREQUENTLY cooked in wood barbecues and smokers. However, as not everyone has these we've adapted the recipe to cook on a more traditional barbecue. Due to their size and the time needed for cooking it isn't practical to cook more than one slab of ribs. However, these are great as an entrée while you cook your other food.

To prepare the ribs wash them in cold water and pat dry with paper towel. If the ribs still have a translucent membrane on the back side you need to remove it. Insert a blunt knife under the membrane then work your fingers under it to loosen it. Grab hold of it using some paper towel for grip and peel it off. Remove any excess fat, this is important to prevent fat fires while cooking.

Combine all the rub ingredients. Rub the ribs all over with the oil, then rub all the spice rub on both sides of the ribs. Cover with foil or plastic wrap and put in the fridge for at least an hour, preferably much longer and up to 24 hours.

Meanwhile, make the sauce. Put the oil in a medium saucepan and heat over medium heat. Add the onion and garlic and cook for 5-10 minutes until softened. Add the tomato paste, red wine, sugar, honey, Worcestershire sauce, vinegar and Tabasco sauce. Stir until the sugar dissolves. Bring to the boil, then simmer for 10-15minutes. Set aside to cool.

Remove the ribs from the fridge 20 minutes before cooking to allow the meat to return to room temperature.

Get your barbecue ready. If possible you should cook the ribs using indirect heat, ie keeping one area much cooler. As the ribs are cooked for a long time, you also want some humidity to prevent them drying out. Put a deepish ovenproof dish (large enough to fit the ribs in) on your barbecue grill and sit a grill rack in it, or on it. Fill the tray ¾ full with water. Heat one side of your barbecue to low, about 110°C (225°F) and try and maintain this temperature all the time, adjusting as necessary.

On a windy day the temperature may fluctuate more. Put the ribs on the rack, meat side up and cook with the hood down for 4½ hours, keeping an eye on the temperature and topping up the water regularly — be careful as if you get a fat build up it may spit when you add more water. Apart from to add water, do not keep opening the lid as you will lose heat.

After about 4½ hours carefully remove the ribs and water bath from the barbecue and increase the heat to medium on both sides. Brush both sides of the ribs with some of the barbecue sauce. Return to the hot barbecue and cook for about 5 minutes (the same way up) with the hood open, ensuring you do not burn the underside. Slice between the ribs and serve with the remaining sauce. Any leftover sauce can be kept in the fridge for up to 7 days and is great with chicken, pork and even in sandwiches!

PREP: 20 minutes, plus overnight marinating if possible
COOK: about 4½ hours
SERVES: 2-6

About 1.5kg slab of spare ribs (American style pork ribs)
1 tablespoon vegetable oil

RUB:
1½ tablespoons brown sugar
1 tablespoon garlic powder
1 tablespoon onion powder
2 teaspoons paprika
1 teaspoon ground black pepper
1 teaspoon ground ginger
½ teaspoon salt

BBQ SAUCE:
1 tablespoon vegetable oil
1 small onion, very finely chopped
4 garlic cloves, crushed
125g (½ cup) tomato paste (puree)
180ml (2/3 cup) red wine
100g brown sugar
1½ tablespoons honey
2 tablespoons Worcestershire sauce
1 tablespoon red wine vinegar
Good dash Tabasco sauce

EXTRA TIPS FOR COOKING RIBS

Never boil or steam the ribs before cooking. This just causes lots of the wonderful flavours to dissolve in the water, never to be tasted again.

If your ribs are particularly fatty you may need to empty the water bath once during cooking. Working quickly but carefully, remove the ribs on the rack and the water bath, close the hood. Tip the water and fat into an ovenproof dish then refill with water and carry on cooking the ribs.

BBQ SAUCE

THIS IS A BARBECUE SAUCE FOR brushing onto meat while it is cooking or for dipping cooked meat and sausages into. It isn't a particularly thick sauce. If you prefer a sweet sauce, add 1-2 tablespoons of sugar. For a more tangy sauce omit the sugar.

Heat the oil in a medium saucepan and add the onion and garlic. Cook over a low heat for 5-10 minutes or until the onion is very soft. Add the remaining ingredients (adding the sugar if you prefer a sweeter sauce), bring to the boil then simmer uncovered for 20-30 minutes, until the sauce has thickened slightly. Remove from the heat and cool. Serve cold.

PREP: 10 minutes
COOK: about 40 minutes
MAKES: 375-500ml (1½ - 2 cups)

1 tablespoon olive oil
1 small onion, finely chopped
2 garlic cloves, crushed
180ml (3/4 cup) tomato sauce (ketchup)
125ml (1/2 cup) orange juice
125ml (1/2 cup) beer
80ml (1/3 cup) honey
80ml (1/3 cup) cider or malt vinegar
2 tablespoons Dijon mustard
4 tablespoons Worcestershire sauce
2 tablespoons brown sugar (optional)

Lots of fun to be had

Real men don't need directions

TAILGATING

AS MY FRIENDS WILL ATTEST, tailgating is one of my favourite barbecue travel stories. Whilst visiting East Lansing, Michigan, good friends of mine Jon and Steph exposed me to an event that continues to bring people back to college, long after they've finished their studies. Tailgating is held in car parks at college football stadiums where people barbecue, drink and party out of the back of their utes/trucks during big college game weekends (Go the Spartans!).

We arrived early, along with many other utes, trucks and campers, to secure our spot. We opened the tailgate of the ute and unloaded eskies, a portable hibachi barbecue, stacks of food, red solo cups, portable camping chairs and ample sporting equipment for the day's festivities.

The car park was an amazing site, ranging from basic utes with small TVs, charcoal hibachis and cans of beer, to the alumni with VIP privileges and expensive toys including huge motor homes/RVs decked out with flat screen TVs, kegs of beer and state of the art barbecues. We even saw a full pig on a spit!

BARBECUE SMOKED SALMON

2 BEER RATING

MUST BE COOKED ON A HOODED OR KETTLE BARBECUE

THIS IS A SIMPLE WAY OF SMOKING your own salmon. You can then eat the salmon as it is, or add it to a variety of other dishes. You'll need to buy some wood chips which you'll find at barbecue stores and home/DIY centers.

Cut four pieces of foil the same width and twice the length as each of your salmon fillets. Fold each piece of foil in half lengthways and sit a fillet, skin-side up on each one. Set aside. This makes the fish more stable on the grill, but the individual pieces of foil still allow the smoke to move around the fish.

Preheat one side of your barbecue to high. Drain the chips then put them into a smoking box or metal tray that can withstand the heat of a barbecue. Put the wood chips on the hot side of the barbie and close the lid. Once you see lots of smoke billowing out of your barbecue, it's time to start smoking! Put the fish (on the foil) on the cold side of the barbie and cook for 30-35 minutes depending on the thickness of the fish. To check if the fish is done, it should flake easily at the thickest part. Serve hot or warm.

Combine the olive oil, vinegar, mustard and salt and pepper and mix well. Just before serving pour over the salad and rocket leaves and toss well. Serve alongside the fish.

For more information on smoking, refer to 'Amsterdam's guide to smoking' page 73.

PREP: 20 minutes
COOK: 30-40 minutes
SERVES: 4

2-3 large handfuls wood smoking chips
4 x 150g salmon fillets, preferably skin-on

Simple green salad:
4 tablespoons good quality olive oil
1½ tablespoons white wine vinegar
2 teaspoons Dijon or wholegrain mustard
Salt and black pepper
50g mixed green salad leaves
50g rocket leaves

Soak the wood chips for between 30 minutes and an hour.

DEATH VALLEY, CALIFORNIA — EARLY BARBECUE IN THE US

IN STRICT CONTRAST TO THE COOL and breezy conditions of California, Death Valley is one of the hottest places in America, and has reached over 50⁰C. Aside from the heat, what caught my attention was the story of an early wagon train in the 1800s that got lost and resulted in one of the first recorded barbecues in the area. Having got lost, the early travellers had to burn the wagon and barbecue their ox as food in order to survive. It's almost as if the importance that barbecuing had to life in Death Valley many years ago is still reflected in the passion the US has for barbecuing to this day.

LA COBB SALAD

I KNEW THERE MUST BE SOMETHING special about this salad when Scotty, a good friend of mine who does everything possible to avoid salads, made a long distance call from LA to rave about it. Invented by Robert Cobb it was a signature menu item of the Hollywood Brown Derby. Variations are now served worldwide but the core ingredients that made it famous include bacon, chicken, egg, Roquefort cheese and the tasty dressing.

Cook the eggs in boiling water for 8 minutes. Plunge into cold water and leave to cool completely. Peel and dice.

Heat the oil in a frying pan over medium-high heat. Add the bacon and fry until crispy. Drain on paper towel, then crumble.

To make the salad, make a bed of the mixed salad leaves and watercress on a serving platter. Arrange the egg, bacon, chicken, avocado, tomato and cheese in a pattern on top, either in rows or in squares like a checkerboard. Scatter the chives over the top.

To make the dressing, whisk together the vinegar, mustard, garlic, Worcestershire sauce and salt and pepper. Mash in the Roquefort cheese, then drizzle in the olive oil whisking until you have a smooth, thick dressing. Drizzle a little over the salad and serve the remaining dressing on the side. If making in advance, do not dress the salad until just before serving.

PREP: 25 minutes
COOK: 10 minutes
SERVES: 4

3 eggs
2 teaspoons vegetable oil
8 bacon slices
100g mixed salad leaves
Small bunch watercress, leaves only
250g cooked chicken, shredded
2 avocados, diced
3 tomatoes, chopped
125g Roquefort cheese, crumbled
1 bunch chives, cut into 5cm (2 in) lengths

Cobb dressing:
2 tablespoons red wine vinegar
½ teaspoon Dijon mustard
1 small garlic clove, crushed
1 teaspoon Worcestershire sauce
Salt and freshly ground black pepper
25g Roquefort cheese, crumbled
100ml olive oil

KEY LIME PIE

IT IS VITAL TO HAVE A BARBECUE thermometer to make this dessert. Brush the base and sides of a 23cm loosed-bottomed flan or cake tin that is at least 7.5cm deep, with a little of the melted butter.

Crush the biscuits into fine crumbs either in a food processor or put them in a ziplock bag and bash with a rolling pin. Put into a large bowl and stir in the melted butter. Mix until well combined. Lightly press into the base of the tin and about 3cm (from the biscuit base) up the side of the tin. Put in the fridge whilst preparing the filling.

Finely grate 2 teaspoons of zest (green bit only) from the limes and squeeze the juice until you have 125ml (½ cup). Preheat your barbecue with the hood down to 350°C (180°F/Gas 4), but if possible leaving one side of the barbecue turned off. Put the egg yolks in

a large bowl and using electric beaters whisk for 2-3 minutes until pale and fluffy. Gradually add the condensed milk, beating well after each addition. Whisk for 4-5 minutes until you have a light, fluffy mixture. Whisk in the lime zest and juice. The mixture will start to thicken immediately.

Immediately pour the filling over the crust and cook on the barbecue, on the cooler side with the hood down for 10 minutes until the filling is set. Remove from the barbecue and cool in the tin on a wire rack. Once cooled completely, remove from the tin (leaving it on the base if it's easier to serve) and transfer to a serving plate.

To make the cream topping, whip the cream until soft peaks form. Add the sugar and beat until stiff, but not solid! Spread over the top of the pie filling and serve cut in wedges.

PREP: 45 minutes
COOK: 10 minutes
SERVES: 8-10

120g unsalted butter, melted
320g graham crackers, granita biscuits or plain digestive biscuits
4 limes (or about 18-20 key limes)
3 large egg yolks
395g can condensed milk

Cream topping
125ml (½ cup) whipping cream
1 tablespoon confectioners' or caster sugar

EUROPE

EUROPEAN BARBECUING IS MORE
about the social occasion –
demonstrating that it is possible to
have true balance between work and
play, with time set aside to savour and
enjoy barbecues properly.

Santorini

GARLIC PRAWNS

TRADITIONALLY THESE PRAWNS are cooked and served in individual terracotta serving dishes swimming in a rich butter and olive oil garlic sauce. However, for making on a barbecue it's easier to serve the garlic butter as a dipping sauce.

For the prawns, put the garlic, oil and lemon juice in a medium-large bowl. Add some salt and pepper and mix well. Add the prawns and toss everything together well. Leave for 10 minutes or so, don't leave for too long or the lemon juice will start to 'cook' the prawns.

Meanwhile to make the sauce, put the oil and butter in a small pan and heat gently until the butter just melts. Add the garlic, chilli flakes and lemon juice and season with salt and pepper. Set aside in the pan.

Cook the prawns on a hot barbecue for about 3 minutes, turning once. Transfer to a serving plate. Quickly reheat the garlic oil, stir in the parsley and serve as a dipping sauce for the prawns, accompanied by plenty of bread for mopping up any sauce.

If preferred, once cooked the prawns can be served in individual dishes with the hot sauce poured over. Once again provide plenty of crusty bread for mopping.

PREP: 40 minutes (mostly peeling prawns)
COOK: 5 minutes
MAKES: 4-6 servings

1 garlic clove, crushed
3 tablespoons olive oil
1 tablespoon lemon juice
750g unpeeled small-medium prawns, peeled, tails left on, deveined
Crusty bread, to serve

GARLIC DIPPING SAUCE:
80ml (1/3 cup) olive oil
40g butter
3 garlic cloves, crushed
¼ teaspoon red chilli flakes
Juice of 1 lemon
Salt and freshly ground black pepper
2 tablespoons chopped fresh parsley

SCALLOPS WITH AVOCADO SALSA

TO MAKE THE AVOCADO SALSA, gently combine the ingredients in a medium bowl. Set aside. Remove the scallops from the shells carefully with a knife. Wash the scallops and the shells then pat dry with paper towel.

Preheat barbecue to high. Brush the scallops on both sides with a little oil and season with salt and pepper. Cook on the barbecue for 2 minutes; then turn and cook for another minute or 2. Return to the washed out shells, add a small spoonful of salsa and serve immediately.

TOP TIP
The easy way to dice an avocado. Using a sharp knife, slice around the avocado from top to bottom. Twist open. Remove the stone with a spoon. Then using a dessert spoon scoop out the halves from the top, so they each come out in one piece. Slice 3 or 4 times lengthways, once horizontally and then 5 or 6 times widthways, trying to keep the half all together while you do this. It should now all be nicely diced.

PREP: 10 minutes
COOK: about 4 minutes
MAKES: 16

16 scallops on the shell
Salt and black pepper

AVOCADO SALSA:
1 large or 2 small ripe avocadoes, diced (see box)
2 tablespoons olive oil, plus extra for brushing
1 tablespoon lemon juice
2 tablespoons chopped flat-leaf parsley

BRUSCETTA

EACH TOPPING MAKES SUFFICIENT to top 6 slices of bread. If making in advance, toast the bread and make the toppings, but don't assemble them until just before serving or they will go soggy.

To make the bruscetta, slice the bread into 12 slices on the diagonal. Toast or barbecue the slices until golden on each side. Lightly squash the garlic with the side of a knife and rub all over the bread. Drizzle one side with oil then top with a topping.

To make the tomato topping, chop 2 of the tomatoes and put in a bowl with the basil, olive oil, sugar and salt and pepper. Mix gently and set aside for 10 minutes. Meanwhile, cut the other tomato in half around the middle and rub it on the oiled sides of 6 slices of toasted bread, squeezing the tomato to extract the juice. Spoon some tomato mixture on top and serve immediately or they will go soggy.

To make the bocconcini topping, preheat barbecue to hot. Cut each capsicum into 3 long flat pieces and remove the seeds and membrane. Brush with olive oil and barbecue skin side down for about 5 minutes, or until the skin blackens and blisters. Put in a plastic bag and leave to cool. Once cool rub off the skin and slice the flesh into thin strips. Top each bruscetta with some slices of bocconcini and red capsicum and a grinding of black pepper.

PREP: 25 minutes
COOK: 5 minutes
MAKES: 12 pieces

BRUSCETTA BASE:
1 crusty Italian loaf, about 35cm long
2 garlic cloves
2 tablespoons olive oil

TOMATO AND BASIL TOPPING:
3 large ripe tomatoes
1 tablespoon roughly torn basil leaves
1 tablespoon olive oil
¼ teaspoon sugar
Salt and black pepper

BOCCONCINI AND RED CAPSICUM TOPPING:
2 small red capsicum
1 tablespoon olive oil
About 180g bocconcini or good quality (ie not rubbery) mozzarella, sliced
Freshly ground black pepper

VENICE

Arriving in Venice I expected to see lots of water beneath my feet, but I didn't expect it to also be falling from the sky. Determined to find Venice's contribution to the world of barbecuing, I forged ahead. After visiting many restaurants around the alleys and canals of Venice, I was impressed by the consistently high quality of the wood-fired pizzas. They had simple Italian toppings enriched by the complex flavours from the wood fire ovens. These traditional wood-fired pizzas were without a doubt Venice's contribution to the world of barbecuing and offered flavours anyone would be proud to call their own.

I smell pizza!

THE EUROPEAN EXPERIENCE

THE EUROPEAN BARBECUE experience exudes a style that sets itself apart from other areas.

Europeans not only create time to barbecue, they prioritise social time above and beyond anything else, allowing ample time to enjoy barbecues. It's not just a passion; it's a way of life.

Perhaps the one exception to this is the UK, constantly at the mercy of the weather. It gets the encouragement award for effort, fighting the elements to barbecue whenever a ray of sunshine appears.

Although traditional barbecues are held regularly throughout Europe, it's where traditional styles and social scenes merge with modern barbecuing that demanded my attention. There are Spanish paellas cooked over wood fires, Italian wood-fired pizzas and breads, Greek and Turkish kebabs and so much more for anyone with an open mind

to barbecuing. And with such a small distance between countries it's possible to enjoy many different experiences within a short period of time.

I've blended the highlights of the favourite foods, locations and experiences here to demonstrate how these come together to show the best Europe has to offer the world of barbecuing.

It's hard to go past the blue Mediterranean waters, white buildings and warm spring weather of Santorini in Greece – unforgettably you can have volcanic ash between your toes whilst cooking on a charcoal barbecue.

As you wait for the barbecue to heat up, it's always nice to enjoy a few refreshing drinks; starting with a selection of Czech beers and French champagne. For those unfamiliar with champagne, it's kind of like premium French beer.

Then, as people start to get

peckish, Spain gives the world tapas – an equivalent social experience to a barbecue – which includes olives, shaved Iberico cured ham, chorizo, barbecued octopus, garlic prawns, scallops, and a selection of Spanish and Italian olive oils with chargrilled dipping bread to warm up the taste buds.

For the main course, there is a selection of barbecued meats and specialty dishes including German bratwurst, Greek souvlaki, and Mediterranean seafood platters with Greek and Caprese salads on the side.

As you enjoy the main meal, it's time to move onto some French Côtes du Rhône wine and the heavy and more flavoursome beers from Belgium.

Finally, after many hours of music, laughing, storytelling and perhaps a mid-afternoon siesta, it's time to indulge those with a sweet tooth. Dessert is a mixture of cakes and sweets from France along with barbecued Brie or Camembert, with a French dessert wine or an Italian digestive such as Limoncello.

MARINATED OLIVES

MIXED OLIVES WITH GARLIC AND CHILLI

To get the best flavour from these olives you should really leave them to marinate for a couple of weeks. But if you don't have time then try and make them a day or 2 in advance. If making them on the day, use only 4 tablespoons of oil. Note that it's normal for the oil to solidify in the fridge. Remove from the fridge an hour or so before serving to allow it to liquify again.

To help the olives absorb more flavour, cut a thin slice around the middle of each one. Put them in a bowl with the garlic, herbs and chillies and mix well. Pack into a 1 litre jar (see box below) and pour over sufficient olive oil to fill. If making in advance, seal and leave to marinate in the fridge for 1-2 weeks and eat within 1 month. If using within 1 week, marinate them for at least 24 hours. Remove from the fridge a few hours before serving to allow the oil to liquefy again. Remove the olives from the oil and serve. The oil can be used for the next day or two for salad dressings and cooking.

GREEN OLIVES WITH CORIANDER AND LEMON

To help the olives absorb more flavour, cut a thin slice around the middle of each one. Put in to a largish bowl. Using a pestle and mortar (or a shatterproof bowl and the end of a rolling pin or wooden spoon) crush the coriander seeds, add to the olives. Thinly slice the lemon, then cut each slice into 6 wedges. Add to the olives with the coriander leaves. Toss everything together well then pack into a 1 litre jar (see box below) and pour over sufficient olive oil to fill. If making in advance, seal and leave to marinate for 1-2 weeks and eat within 1 month. If using within 1 week, marinate them for at least 24 hours. Remove from the fridge a few hours before serving to allow the oil to liquefy again. At a pinch these could be made on the day, as the flavours are quite strong. Use only 4 tablespoons of oil.

MIXED OLIVES WITH GARLIC AND CHILLI

PREP: 30 minutes (plus time to sterilize jars). Makes enough to fill a 1 litre jar.

500g mixed olives, such as Ligurian, kalamata and green olives
3 garlic cloves, thinly sliced
1 tablespoon fresh oregano leaves (or 1 teaspoon dried oregano)
2 sprigs fresh thyme
2 small red chillies, seeded and sliced
About 500ml (2 cups) olive oil

GREEN OLIVES WITH CORIANDER AND LEMON

PREP: 30 minutes (plus time to sterilize jars). Makes enough to fill a 1 litre jar.

The smell of crushed coriander seeds, freshly sliced lemon and coriander is intoxicating.

500g large green olives
2 teaspoons coriander seeds
½ lemon
2 tablespoons chopped fresh coriander leaves
About 500ml (2 cups) olive oil

TOP TIP

To sterlise glass jars. If you want to keep these olives for longer than a week and up to one month, you will need to store them in sterilised jars in the fridge. Sterilising is easy. Preheat oven to 170°C (335°F/Gas 3). Take a 1 litre glass jar with a wide neck and close fitting lid and wash and rinse the jar and lid in hot water. Dry well with a clean tea towel, then put in the oven for 10 minutes. Turn the oven off but leave the jars in the oven keeping warm until you use them.

Is there a barbecue on I don't know about?

A humble backyard barbecue by the sea

CAPRESE SALAD

A DELICIOUS TASTING AND beautiful looking salad from the Campania region of Italy. It's really worth buying good quality buffalo mozzarella and decent tomatoes for this salad.

Arrange alternate slices of tomato, mozzarella and basil leaves in a circle on a serving dish. Drizzle with the olive oil and season with salt and freshly ground black pepper.

This can be made an hour or so in advance, then kept covered in the fridge. Allow to come to room temperate before serving.

PREP: 15 minutes
SERVES: 6

About 4 ripe, firm tomatoes, cut into 1cm (½ in) thick slices
250g buffalo mozzarella, cut in 5mm thick slices
Handful small fresh basil leaves
1½ - 2 tablespoons good quality extra virgin olive oil
Sea salt and freshly ground black pepper

How to roast in Spain

Hmm ... so many choices

Champagne – it's like fancy beer

I Louvre barbecuing

GAZPACHO

TO COPE WITH THE SEARING HEAT of the summers, the Spanish eat chilled soups, with gazpacho being one of the most famous.

Cut a cross into the bottom of each tomato. Put into a bowl of boiling water for about 10 seconds, then plunge into cold water. Remove from the water and peel off the skins. Halve, deseed and roughly chop.

Soak the bread in a little bit of water for 5 minutes, then squeeze it out. Put into a blender with the onion and garlic and a little salt and pepper. Whiz until pureed. Set aside 2 tablespoons of the red capsicum to use as a garnish. Add the remainder to the blender with the tomatoes, cucumber, red capsicum and vinegar and puree until smooth or until of a consistency of your liking. With the motor running gradually add the oil. Refrigerate for several hours, or freeze for 30 minutes.

Chop the reserved capsicum into small dice and put the garnishes into individual serving bowls. Stir 80ml (1/3 cup) iced water into the soup. Mix well and serve the soup very chilled accompanied by the garnishes.

TOP TIP
To deseed a cucumber, halve it lengthways, then use a teaspoon to scrape out the seeds.

PREP: 30 minutes
SERVES 4

4 firm, ripe tomatoes
2 slices of crusty bread, crusts removed
1 small onion, finely chopped
1 small garlic clove, crushed
Salt and freshly ground black pepper
1 large red capsicum, deseeded and chopped
1 small cucumber (about 100g), peeled, halved, deseeded and chopped (see box)
2 tablespoons red wine vinegar
2 tablespoons olive oil

TO GARNISH:
½ small red onion, finely diced
1 small cucumber, deseeded and finely diced

GREEK CHICKEN SKEWERS WITH COUNTRY SALAD

SERVE UP THESE SIMPLE CHICKEN skewers and a Horiatiki Salata (Greek country salad) then sit back and drift away to the whitewashed houses, cobbled streets and simple tavernas of the Greek island of your dreams.

If using wooden skewers, soak them in water for at least an hour to prevent them burning.

Put all the kebab ingredients (except the chicken) in a small bowl and whisk well to combine. Put the cubed chicken in a bowl, pour over the marinade and mix well ensuring all the chicken is evenly coated. Set aside to marinate for at least 2 hours and up to 24 hours.

Remove from the fridge 30 minutes before using.

Drain the chicken reserving the marinade, then thread onto the skewers. Cook on a medium-hot barbecue for 8-10 minutes, basting with the reserved marinade and turning 3–4 times, being careful not to burn the outside while leaving the inside raw! Serve accompanied by the Greek salad.

To make the salad, combine the tomatoes, cucumber, capsicum, onion and olives in a bowl. Scatter the feta and oregano (if using) over the top, add some black pepper then drizzle the oil over the top.

PREP: 45 minutes
COOK: (about) 8-10 minutes
MAKES: 8 skewers

CHICKEN KEBABS:
8 wooden or metal skewers
3 tablespoons (60ml/¼ cup) olive oil
3 tablespoons (60ml/¼ cup) fresh lemon juice
1-2 garlic cloves, crushed
½ teaspoon ground cumin
½ teaspoon paprika
Salt and black pepper
700g (about 3) chicken breast, cut into 3cm (1-inch) squares

HORIATIKI SALATA, TO SERVE 4:
2 large firm, ripe tomatoes, halved and cut into wedges
2 small cucumbers, peeled and thinly sliced
1 green capsicum (pepper), deseeded and thinly sliced into rings
½ small red onion, thinly sliced into rings
100g pitted kalamata olives
200g feta cheese, crumbled
1 tsp dried oregano (optional)
Freshly ground black pepper
4 tablespoons (80ml/1/3 cup) good quality olive oil

These rocks are hot enough to barbecue on

An ancient Greek barbecue area?

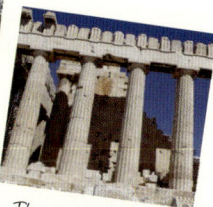
They sure built their barbecues fancy!

VERY SIMPLE EASTERN EUROPEAN CABBAGE SALAD

SHRED THE CABBAGE AS FINELY AS possible (discarding the hard core) and put into a large bowl. Add the vinegar and 250ml (1 cup) of water and mix gently. Put a small plate on top of the cabbage to keep it submerged and leave for an hour in the fridge.

Drain well then drizzle over the oil and plenty of black pepper and mix well. If you like quite a sour taste add a splash more vinegar, but it is not vital. Serve.

PREP: 10 minutes (plus chilling)
SERVES: 6-8

300g (about half a small) white cabbage
250ml (1 cup) white vinegar
1 tablespoon olive oil
Freshly ground black pepper

TURKISH LAMB KEBABS

PUT A SIEVE OVER A SMALL BOWL and squeeze the tomato into the sieve. Then put the squashed tomato into the sieve and press down on it to extract the juice. Discard the squashed tomato. (If using tomato juice instead just put it in a bowl.) Add the olive oil, oregano, lemon juice, garlic, one torn bay leaf and salt and pepper to the to-mato juice and mix well. Put the lamb in a bowl, pour over the marinade and mix well, ensuring all the meat is well coated. Leave to marinate in the fridge for at least 2 hours and up to 12.

If using wooden skewers, soak them in water for at least an hour, or while preparing the kebabs.

Drain the lamb, reserving the marinade for basting. Thread the lamb onto the kebabs, threading 1 bay leaf around the middle piece of meat on each kebab.

Cook on a hot barbecue for 6-8 minutes, turning regularly and basting with the marinade. The cooking time will vary from barbecue to barbecue, but you want the meat nice and brown on the outside but still pink on the inside.

If serving with the pitta bread, toast both sides lightly on the barbecue then slice open. Combine the tomato, onion and parsley in a serving dish and drizzle with a little olive oil. To serve, spoon some tomato salad into a pitta bread and top with the lamb.

PREP: 45 minutes
MAKES: 10 kebabs

1 large ripe tomato, quartered (or 3 table-spoons tomato juice)
10 wooden or metal skewers
125ml (½ cup) olive oil (plus extra for drizzling)
2 teaspoons dried oregano
juice of 1 small lemon (about 3 table-spoons)
11 bay leaves
2 garlic cloves, crushed
Salt and black pepper
700g lamb fillet, cut into 2-3cm cubes

TO SERVE (OPTIONAL, BUT DELICIOUS)
4-5 pitta bread
3 tomatoes, finely chopped
1 small red onion, finely chopped
Handful flat-leaf parsley leaves, roughly torn

SEVILLE, SOUTH OF SPAIN

Finding a tapas restaurant in Seville required some careful navigation around the labyrinthine alleys that wind through the centre of town. Partially disorientated, I sat at a little restaurant and ordered an icy cold Cruzcampo beer, a plate of cured ham (jamón), and a bowl of green olives to curb my appetite while I waited for fellow patrons to arrive.

Sitting alone, staring in amaze-ment at the jamón hanging from hooks above the bar, I wondered if I had chosen the most unpopular restaurant in Spain. The food was great and the beer was cold, so how could this be? Then, like magic, by my second round of tapas, I looked up with amazement and every seat was full. The Spanish often eat after 9 pm when the day has cooled down. So be prepared for some late night barbecues.

Tapas is Spain's version of local barbecue. Like a barbie, they offer the perfect environment to socialise, eat and drink outdoors. The small tapas plates are perfectly suited to the hot climate where you can nibble at many different flavours without overfilling, allowing you to prolong the enjoy-ment as long as humanly possible.

My tapas favourites include garlic prawns, meat balls, chorizo, omelette, jamón and marinated olives. They not only taste great but promote even greater social interaction and a fun style of eating at the barbecue.

LEANING BARBECUE HAM AND MUSHROOM PIZZA ITALY

MUST BE COOKED ON A HOODED OR KETTLE BARBECUE

MAKES 2 PIZZAS BUT FOR BEST results cook one at a time.

These pizzas need to be cooked over indirect heat so you don't just blacken the bottom. So heat up your barbecue and put the hood down while you prepare the pizzas. With a charcoal barbecue preheat the coals for about 45 minutes, then just before you put the pizza on, put a baking tray on the coals but underneath the grill.

Melt the butter in a saucepan over medium heat. Add 1 clove of crushed garlic and the mushrooms. Cook for 2 minutes until the mushrooms are starting to soften.

Stir the remaining garlic and crushed red chillies into the pizza sauce. Spread over the pizza bases, then scatter over the mozzarella cheese. Top with the mushrooms and any buttery juices and the ham.

Once the barbecue is up to about 200°C (or feels pretty hot) put the pizza on and lower the hood. Turn off the heat under the pizza (but leaving the other burners on) and leave to cook for 8-10 minutes or until the cheese melts and the base is golden, not blackened. If cooking the second pizza straight away, turn the burner back on for 2 minutes to reheat, then turn it off and cook the pizza as above. Serve immediately topped with rocket leaves, if using.

PREP: 20-25 minutes
COOK: about 12 minutes per pizza
MAKES: 2 big pizzas, about 30cm in diameter

1 knob of butter
3 garlic cloves, crushed
200g button or brown mushrooms, sliced
½ teaspoon crushed red chillies
About 300g pizza sauce
2 large pizza bases about 30cm in diameter
250g grated mozzarella cheese
200g ham, roughly chopped
75g rocket leaves, to serve (optional)

Pizza in Piza

WHY REAL MEN EAT SALAD

I have had countless arguments with real men regarding the question of whether real men eat salads. After a recent trip to Ios, I believe I have the definitive answer.

I arrived in Ios to join Travis, a good friend of mine who had travelled there a few months earlier for a short getaway, but couldn't bring himself to leave. As friends do, I was happy to go along with the flow and joined his daily routine of partying at night and sleeping on the beach during the day. Our daily meal was a tasty, yet vitamin deficient meat-only Gyro kebab. Seriously, when meat tastes that good, who needs to eat salad?

Well, it turns out Trav needed to. Having left the island, I later heard he had visited the local doctor and was told he had a modern day case of scurvy! A reminder to all real men out there: don't avoid the salads, or at least don't forget your vitamin C!

MARINATED PORK WITH BALSAMIC RED ONIONS

THIS IS BETTER COOKED UNDER a hood, but if you don't have one you can still do it, just cook the pork for a little longer, ensuring you don't burn the outside. The onions need to be cooked on a flat plate. If you don't have one, either put a frying pan on the barbie or cook the onions in the kitchen.

Combine the red wine, bay leaves, thyme and garlic and season with black pepper. Put the pork in a medium dish and pour the marinade over, turn it a couple of times, cover and refrigerate for at least an hour and up to 24 hours. Remove from the fridge 20 minutes before cooking, to return to room temperature.

Meanwhile, halve the onions (keeping the root on to help keep the onion together) then cut each half into 4 long wedges. Put in a bowl and toss in 1 tablespoon of the oil and some salt and pepper. Combine the remaining oil with the balsamic vinegar. Wash the rocket leaves, pat dry then put in a bowl and into the fridge.

Preheat barbecue to medium, preferably the hot plate but a grill will also work and put the hood down. Remove the pork from the marinade (reserving the marinade for basting) and pat dry. Cook for about 15 minutes with the hood down, turning regularly and basting with the marinade. Do not baste the final time of turning. Transfer to a plate, cover and leave to rest for 5 minutes. Slice thickly.

While the pork is resting, put the onions on the barbecue flat plate and cook (hood up) for about 5 minutes, turning regularly until slightly blackened. Pour over the balsamic dressing and cook for a minute or two. Gently toss the onions through the rocket leaves. Serve the pork accompanied by the onions and rocket.

PREP: 10 minutes
COOK: 20 minutes
SERVES: 4 (this recipe can easily be doubled to serve 8, just use two 750g pieces of pork)

300ml red wine
2 bay leaves, torn
2 thyme sprigs, broken up
2 garlic cloves, crushed
Salt and freshly ground black pepper
750g piece pork fillet
2 red onions
2 tablespoons olive oil
1 tablespoon balsamic vinegar
100g rocket leaves

BEST BEERS AT A EUROPEAN BARBECUE

Even before arriving in Europe, I was familiar with a number of the flavoursome local beers – beers that are so good they're enjoyed at barbecues all around the world.

I guess their popularity isn't overly surprising when you consider Germany is home to the world's famous Oktoberfest beer festival, that Ireland created Guinness and Belgium has Trappist monks dedicating their time to creating the perfect drop.

Being an informal affair, many excuses are acceptable when arriving late to a barbecue, but one of the most used excuses is real men underestimating the time required to browse the bottle shop before making the important decision of which beers to bring along.

In Belgium, this problem was amplified. Rather than dozens, there were hundreds of world-class beers. Needless to say, I was extremely late to my first barbecue in Brussels, but, at least arrived beers in hand.

AMSTERDAM'S GUIDE TO SMOKING

TO BE CLEAR, THE SMOKING technique is an adaption from the United States and Australia who have really mastered the art of smoking meat. However, let's face it, Amsterdam still retains the title of the ultimate smoking city, as they are willing to smoke almost anything – but that's a topic for another book.

Smoking is the process by which different types of hardwood are added to the cooking process, to create new and complementary flavours – where there's smoke, there's flavour. My favourite woods for

smoking include oak, apple, hickory, maple and whatever hardwood the local area has to offer. The wood chips should be soaked in cold water for 30 minutes prior to cooking, ensuring the wood doesn't instantly catch on fire, but rather smokes as it is intended.

To smoke you need a smoker, hooded barbecue, charcoal kettle or basically anything that's capable of retaining heat and smoke for extended periods. Ideally the temperatures are maintained at 120-150 degrees Celsius for extended cooking, or higher

temperatures if you're cooking for shorter periods.

Typically smoking is a low heat and slow cooking approach, so in an attempt to generate high levels of flavour, don't fall into the trap of using too much smoke – over-smoking can result in a bitter taste. Start with just a handful at a time, each hour. Experiment with the different combinations of wood and cooking times to become a professional in your own right.

GRILLED OCTOPUS

IN GREECE A WHOLE OCTOPUS WOULD be more traditional, but baby octopus are more easily available and not quite so daunting to cook.

If you didn't buy cleaned octopus, you'll need to clean the guts out. Even if you've bought cleaned ones there's still a bit of preparation that needs to be done.

First off use a sharp knife to cut between the head and the tentacle section, just below the eyes. Then cut the tentacles in half lengthways and pop out the beak-thing. Rinse the tentacles under cold water. Snip the tips off the tentacles and if the octopuses are particularly large cut the tentacles in half again. Now, back to the head. Make a careful slit down one side of it – trying to avoid the ink sac – and scrape out all the insides, including the ink sac. Open it out flat and rinse under cold water.

Remove the eyes by slicing off a thin disc and discarding. Then pull off the thin skin, once again under running water. OK you are ready to go.

Combine the remaining ingredients then pour over the octopus. Mix well to ensure they are evenly coated then leave to marinate in the fridge for at least 1 hour and up to 6 hours.

Remove from the fridge 20 minutes before cooking and remove from the marinade, shaking off any excess marinade. Reserve the marinade. Preheat barbecue to high. Put the reserved marinade in a small saucepan and bring to the boil. Boil for 2-3 minutes until it is slightly syrupy, then remove from the heat.

Barbecue the octopus for 2-3 minutes, turning once or until they are cooked through and curly. Pour the marinade over and serve, accompanied by a green salad.

PREP: 15 minutes if octopus are already cleaned
COOK: 2-3 minutes
SERVES: 4-6

1kg baby octopus, preferably cleaned (ask your fishmonger to do this)
125ml (½ cup) olive oil
4 garlic cloves, crushed
1 tablespoon dried oregano
Juice of 1 lemon
2 tablespoons red wine or red wine vinegar
Salt and freshly ground black pepper
Green salad, to serve

CURED HAMS OF MADRID SPAIN

There are many examples on my travels where pork has been central to a great barbecue. From pork shoulder, to ribs, whole hogs, Christmas hams and trusty old bacon. However, I still wondered if there was something else out there, yet to be discovered.

Well, it took a trip to Madrid to find out. On behalf of the world of barbecuing, I would like to claim cured ham, jamón, as an honorary member of the barbecue family.

Although it's not technically barbecue food, it has many of the vital elements. It's great tasting, it's prepared by real men who have a passion for great food and are willing to spend the time required to produce spectacular results. And while it's being prepared and cured it leaves ample social time with friends.

Tip: A good friend from Madrid, Antonio, insists that this honorary barbecue delight must be eaten with your hands to be truly appreciated – try it for yourself and see!

STEAMING GARLIC AND WINE MUSSELS

AS THERE'S A FAIR BIT OF WINE AND cream involved in this recipe you need to cook this in a pan on your barbecue. Of course, you can also make this on your stove top. This is also delicious cooked with clams instead of mussels, or even a mixture of both.

Scrub the mussels under cold running water to remove any dirt and pull off the hairy beard that protrudes. Tap any open ones on the work top and if they don't close, discard them.

Preheat barbecue to hot. Put a large pan on the barbecue and get it hot.

Add the oil, onion, garlic and thyme and cook, stirring regularly for about 5 minutes until the onion softens. Add the mussels and shake the pan about a bit. Add the wine, then put lid on and cook for 3-4 minutes or until the mussels have opened, shaking the pan occasionally. Pour in the cream, add the parsley and mix everything together well then serve immediately, discarding any unopened mussels. Serve in bowls, ensuring everyone gets plenty of the creamy sauce. Serve accompanied by crusty bread for mopping up the sauce.

PREP: 15-20 minutes
COOK: about 8 minutes
SERVES: 4

1.75kg small mussels
1 tablespoon olive oil
1 small onion, finely chopped
4 garlic cloves, finely chopped
1 thyme sprig (optional)
125ml (1/2 cup) dry white wine or sparkling wine
80ml (1/3 cup) cream
Small handful flat-leaf parsley leaves, roughly chopped
Crusty bread, to serve

CHARGRILLED VEG PASTA SALAD

THE BEAUTY OF THIS DISH IS THAT the flavours continue to develop the longer it sits. So it's perfect for taking on a walk, heading down to the beach or to have ready for once you've set up your camp.

Preheat barbecue to medium-hot. Put the zucchini, capsicum and red onion into a large bowl. Drizzle over 2 tablespoons of the oil, season well with salt and black pepper, then toss everything about to coat well in oil. Chargrill on the barbie until soft, about 1-2 minutes on each side for the zucchini and onion and a little longer for the capsicum. You may well have to do this in a couple of batches.

Cook the pasta until al dente, according to the packet instructions. Drain.

Cool the vegetables slightly then chop everything into bite-sized pieces and gently mix into the cooked pasta with the herbs. Combine the remaining oil with the garlic, chilli and lemon juice and gently stir into the pasta. Transfer to an airtight container and refrigerate until heading out on your walk. If serving at home, chill until needed.

TOP TIP

For meat lovers you could also add some chopped ham or some cooked bacon, sausages or chicken. However, if transporting this for longer than 20 minutes, make sure it is kept well chilled to prevent any possible food poisoning.

PREP: 40 minutes
COOK: about 10 minutes
SERVES: 4-6

2 medium zucchini, cut into 5mm slices lengthways
1 large red capsicum, seeded and cut into thick slices
1 red onion, halved (keeping root intact) and sliced into thin wedges
4 tablespoons (80ml/1/3 cup) olive oil
Salt and freshly ground black pepper
280g pasta shapes
2 tablespoons chopped fresh mint
2 tablespoons chopped fresh parsley
1 big garlic clove, crushed
1 red chilli, seeded and finely chopped
1 tablespoon fresh lemon juice

GREEK STUFFED ROASTED CAPSICUM

TO MAKE THE FILLING, HEAT THE OIL in a large saucepan or frying pan. Add the onion, garlic and celery and sauté over gently heat for 5 minutes. Add the carrot and cook for another couple of minutes. Move the vegetables to one side of the pan, increase the heat and add the mince. Fry until browned. Stir everything together again and add the oregano, tomatoes, red wine (if using) and mushrooms and bring to the boil. Reduce the heat and simmer covered for 20 minutes. Remove the lid and simmer for a further 10-15 minutes to allow the excess liquid to evaporate and the sauce to thicken.

Meanwhile, preheat barbecue to medium-low with the hood down. Slice the tops off the capsicums about 2cm down, reserving the lids. Remove any seeds and membrane. Put the capsicums with their lids on on the barbecue (standing up) and close the hood and cook for about 15 minutes.

Remove from the barbecue and tip out any liquid, spoon in the filling and replace the lids. Cook with the hood down for about 5-10 minutes.

TOP TIP
You can easy make these using any leftover bolognaise sauce. If you have any cooked rice you can add that too. Make sure you heat the sauce thoroughly before spooning into the capsicums.

MUST BE COOKED ON A HOODED OR KETTLE BARBECUE

PREP: 25 minutes
COOK: about 55 minutes
MAKES: 6

1 tablespoon olive oil
1 onion, finely chopped
2 garlic cloves, crushed
2 celery stalks, finely chopped
1 carrot, finely chopped
400g lamb or beef mince
1 teaspoon dried oregano
400g can chopped tomatoes
125ml (½ cup) red wine (optional)
100g button mushrooms, finely chopped
6 medium red capsicum

TARTE TARTIN

PEEL, CORE AND QUARTER THE apples, then slice each quarter in half again lengthways. Put the butter and sugar into a deepish 25cm heavy based frying pan that has a heatproof handle (if you're not sure about the handle wrap it in foil). Cook over low-medium heat, stirring occasionally until the butter and sugar have melted. This will take 5-10 minutes. Remove from the heat and neatly arrange the apples in circles, packing them in one by one. Try and keep them neat as the tart will be turned out, so the apples will be the top.

Return to low-medium heat for about 30-40 minutes and cook until the apples are just soft and the butter and sugar have caramelized around them. Brush the apples with some of the caramel while they are cooking. Once cooked, there should be no excess liquid. However, some apples produce more liquid than others, if you do have excess liquid carefully spoon it off, trying to leave the buttery caramel in the pan. Remove from the heat.

Preheat oven to 190°C (375°F/Gas 5). While the apples are cooking, roll the pastry out to a circle approximately 28cm in diameter, if using pre-rolled, ensure it is 28cm, if not roll it out further. Carefully lay the pastry over the top of the apples, tucking the pastry inside the pan. Bake for 25-30 minutes until the pastry is golden. Sit for 5 minutes then carefully turn out onto a serving plate, replacing any apples that stick to the pan. Serve with whipped cream or ice-cream.

PREP: 25 minutes
COOK: about 1 hour 20 minutes
SERVES: 6-8

1kg firm dessert apples, such as Granny Smith
70g unsalted butter
185g (3/4 cup) caster sugar
350g shortcrust pastry, or 1 large pre-rolled sheet
Whipped cream or ice-cream, to serve

SOUTH AMERICA

SOUTH AMERICA CONTINUES
to produce some of the world's
best barbecuing through the use of
traditional wood fire techniques and
simple seasoning (aka lots of salt),
showing that barbecues don't need to
be complicated.

An icy margarita, anyone?

ASADO DE TIRA WITH PEBRE SAUCE

2 BEER RATING

MUST BE COOKED ON A HOODED BARBECUE

PEBRE SAUCE IS A TRADITIONAL HOT chilli sauce from Chile which is made both with and without tomatoes. This sauce is also fabulous served as an accompaniment to chicken and many other beef dishes.

If you have a small food processor, put the garlic, spring onions, vinegar, chilli, coriander, salt and pepper in the bowl and puree until smooth. Transfer to a bowl and stir in the tomatoes and olive oil and stir again. Set aside for at least an hour to allow the flavours to develop. If you don't have a food processor, whisk the oil and vinegar together until combined then add the remaining ingredients.

Wash the ribs and pat dry with paper towel. Rub all over with the salt and set aside for 20 minutes, not in the fridge.

You need to cook the ribs by indirect heat. If you have 3 or 4 burners, turn on the outside 2 only or if you only have 2 turn on one side only. Fill an ovenproof dish with water and sit it on the barbecue. This helps to keep the ribs moist while they cook. Top it up as necessary while the ribs cook.

Put the ribs on the cooler part of the barbecue and cook for 1 hour with the hood down. Turn over and cook for a further 30 minutes, if they are too brown wrap them in foil. Remove from the heat, cover and leave for 20 minutes.

Serve the sauce at room temperature as an accompaniment to the ribs.

TOP TIP
Beef ribs should be easily available at your butchers. They are known variously as Argentinean or asado ribs or short ribs.

PREP: 15 minutes
COOK: (about) 1½ - 2 hours
SERVES: 4

2 garlic cloves, crushed
4 spring onions, finely chopped
2 tablespoons red wine vinegar
1 haberno (or similar) hot chili, seeded and chopped
1 coriander, leaves only, finely chopped
Salt and freshly ground black pepper
2 medium firm, ripe tomatoes, diced
60ml (¼ cup) olive oil
About 1.3kg short cut beef ribs (see box)
Sea salt

A chilly barbecue in Chile

Not much room for a backyard barbie!

SPICY SALSA & CORN CHIPS

1 BEER RATING

COMBINE ALL THE INGREDIENTS, except the corn chips and adjust the lime juice and chilli to suit your taste.

Put into a serving bowl and serve accompanied by the corn chips.

This is great served as a starter while you're cooking other food. Or serve it alongside steak, sausages or simple grilled fish to liven a dish up. Perfect to serve with the fajitas on page 96.

PREP: 15 minutes
SERVES 4 (just double the quantities to serve more)

4 medium tomatoes, finely chopped
1 small red onion, finely chopped
About 2 tablespoons lime juice
3 tablespoons chopped fresh coriander leaves
1-2 small red chillies, seeded and finely chopped
Good quality corn chips, to serve

The barbecue Gods look over us!

Our great barbecue restaurant, Lapena

Everything in South America is colourful

One too many beers

CHILE STREET VENDOR NUTS

2 BEER RATING

Preheat to 180°C (350°F/Gas 4). Remove any visible loose skins from the peanuts. Put the sugar and 80ml (1/3 cup) water in a heavy based frying pan over low-medium heat. Heat gently until the sugar dissolves, stirring occasionally using a wooden (not metal) spoon. Add the peanuts, mix well and continue to cook over medium heat (the mixture should be bubbling), stirring often for about 10 minutes until the peanuts are coated with the sticky syrup and there is no excess syrup left. Quickly tip onto a baking sheet and spread apart.

Cook for 20 minutes. Remove and carefully break up the pieces with a spoon. Set aside to cool. Once cooled, sprinkle with salt if liked or serve as they are. If not eating immediately store in an airtight container.

TOP TIP

To clean a pan that has been used to make caramel, put it on the stove top and add a splash of orange juice and washing up liquid. Add some water and bring slowly to the boil, stirring with a scrubbing brush. The caramel should all dissolve. Rinse under cold water.

PREP: 5-10 minutes
COOK: 35 minutes

300g (2 cups) raw, shelled (but skins on) peanuts
140g (1/3 cup) granulated sugar
Sea salt, optional

Fresh seafood close at hand in Mexico

ADVENTURES IN SOUTH AMERICAN BARBECUING

Mexico and South America destroy any pre-conceived ideas of barbecuing upon arrival, only to replace them with something unexpected.

Mexico has such a diverse range of backyards for the avid barbecue enthusiast that go well beyond Coronas and sombreros. A barbecue in Mexico is an experience that stays with you for many years to come – that is, if you are able to leave in the first place.

Day one, I was ankle deep in the powder soft sand of Tulum enjoying seafood straight from the crystal-clear ocean cooked on a makeshift beach barbecue.

The next day, I was sitting in a jungle in the shadow of the ancient Mayan temples of Palenque drinking Coronas by the hypnotic light of fire dancers and unexpectedly enjoying

a wood-fired pizza called 'Toxica' that rivals the best in Italy.

Unlike the plastic Tex-Mex, true Mexican fare, like the people, is more laid back and relaxed. It includes local meat and seafood if close to the coastline, with tortillas (tor-tias), spicy tomato salsa, red hot chillies (habanero if you're game) and black beans providing the basis for many meals.

Moving south, I visited a true barbecuing heavyweight contender: Argentina! A long-time favourite of mine, Argentina always delivers. A bulging stomach, aching jaw, and clogged intestines are all signs it's time to leave. Your mind is sending out hints to leave, but your taste buds keep crying out for just one more mouth-watering parrilla, washed down by a local Malbec wine.

In Brazil I did what any barbecue enthusiast does – I visited a churrascaria, a Portuguese barbecue, for a primal meat-easting experience.

South America offers too many experiences for one book, but be sure to finish your South American barbecue experience with desserts from Uruguay, the sweet-tooth capital of South America.

BUENOS AIRES CHIMICHURI

IT IS PREFERABLE TO MAKE THIS sauce in a food processor, but if you don't have one just chop the parsley very finely and combine with the remaining ingredients.

Put the parsley in a food processor and process briefly. Add the remaining ingredients and process to a smooth consistency. Cut 2 or 3 shallow slices across each steak. Put into a shallow dish and pour over half the sauce, rubbing it all over the meat and into the cuts. Leave to marinate in the fridge for at least 2 hours and up to 6 hours. Put the remaining sauce in the fridge too.

Remove the meat and sauce from the fridge 20 minutes before cooking to return to room temperature. Remove the beef from the sauce and allow any excess to drip off.

Grill over medium-high heat for 2 minutes, turn over and grill for a further 1 minute until medium-rare or cooked to your liking. The cooking time will depend on the thickness of your steak and your barbecue. Carve the steak immediately across the grain into strips about 5mm thick and serve accompanied by the extra sauce. Do not allow the meat to sit before serving or it may toughen.

PREP: 20 minutes
COOK: about 3 minutes
SERVES: 4

900kg (2 lb) flank steak

MARINADE/SAUCE:
1 bunch flat leaf parsley, roughly chopped
4 garlic cloves, crushed
125ml (½ cup) olive oil
60ml (¼ cup) red wine vinegar
1 teaspoon dried crushed red pepper flakes
1 teaspoon black pepper
½ teaspoon salt
1 shallot (eschallot), finely chopped
1 teaspoon dried oregano

EL CALAFATE, ARGENTINA — PATAGONIAN LAMB

El Calafate is the gateway town to Los Glaciares National Park, in the southern region of Argentina named Patagonia. A day trip from El Calafate reveals the Perito Moreno Glacier standing over 60 metres high. It is a translucent aqua blue with jagged edges that frequently crash into the surrounding icy waters.

In this region, snow capped mountains and glaciers are a common site, but more importantly it is home to the world famous, Patagonian lamb. Benchmarks are set high in El Calafate and comparing Patagonian lamb to a normal lamb cutlet is like comparing the nearby Moreno Glacier to an ice cube.

The Patagonian lamb is unlike any-thing I've tasted or experienced. Walk-ing into the local parrilla restaurant,

it was apparent we were in for a treat. Standing almost religiously in the garage-sized walk-in barbecue oven were multiple lambs stretched out in cross formation – a common practice in Patagonia.

When the meal arrived, my first thought was, 'Wow, that doesn't look like it came off a supermarket shelf.' Then, 'I wonder what part this

is?' My final thought was, 'This is the best lamb I've ever tasted'. There is something real about the experience of eating food that still resembles part of the gracious animal from which it came.

The lamb was beautifully accom-panied by a silky smooth Malbec red wine, grown in the high country of Mendoza, but that's another story.

I think the owners of 'The BBQ Kings of South America' restaurant thought I was crazy, standing in the oven, trying to work out the best way to capture this amazing scene, before my camera and I started to roast like the lamb! Apologies for the quality of the photo – taking photos from inside a barbecue isn't something I've had a lot of practice at.

ISLA MUJERES (ORANGE FISH)

PUT THE ANNATTO, CORIANDER, peppercorns, cumin, cloves and oregano in a spice grinder and grind to a fine powder, this may take a while as annatto seeds are very hard.

Put the garlic in a small bowl, add the salt and crush to a paste. Gradually work in the spice powder. Add the orange and lime or grapefruit juice and mix to a smooth paste.

Rub all over the fish and leave to marinate in the fridge for about 4 hours. The paste looks pretty thick and overwhelming, but don't worry it tastes great.

Cook over a medium barbecue for about 8-10 minutes, turning once, the exact cooking time will depend on the thickness of the fish, so be careful not to overcook it. To check that it is cooked, the flesh should flake close to the bone. Serve accompanied by salad.

TOP TIP

If you don't want to use mackerel, this dish is traditionally cooked using red snapper or sea bream so try them instead. You can also use fish fillets, no problem.

PREP: 25 minutes
COOK: 10 minutes
SERVES: 4

1½ tablespoons annatto seeds (also called achiote seeds)
½ tablespoon coriander seeds
½ tablespoon black peppercorns
½ teaspoon cumin seeds
3 cloves
2 teaspoons dried oregano
5 garlic cloves, halved
1 teaspoon salt
1½ tablespoons orange juice
1½ tablespoons lime or grapefruit juice
4 whole mackerel, scaled, fins removed, cleaned or 4 mackerel fillets (or see box for alternative fish)

Beach barbie, anyone?

TULUM, MEXICO – WHERE IS EVERYONE?

Often overshadowed by its attention-seeking sibling, Cancun, Tulum has all the looks and charm – bright blue Caribbean waters that wash onto talcum powder soft sand.

Each morning the coastline is scattered with fishing boats providing a constant supply of fresh fish to the locals. One morning, I excitedly grabbed two fish in expectation of a barbecue feast with new friends. Then, to my dismay, at the end of the day all the tourists had returned to their buses and I was left with the sounds of the ocean and the watching eyes of the local iguanas as I barbecued my two fish, all alone.

As I cooked – for one – a question crossed my mind. Is a 'barbecue', still referred to as a barbecue if no-one is around to share it with you?

PUERTO ESCONDIDO, OAXACA – BEST BEERS FOR A MEXICAN BARBECUE

Mexican beers have a light and crisp taste and, when they are served with a slice of fresh lime, or as the locals say it 'lemon', provide the perfect refreshment for the hot and humid weather. I visited Puerto Escondido during a local holiday period and, as you would expect, families flocked to the beaches to enjoy great food and cold beers.

I lined up alongside the holiday-makers at a rusty old charcoal barbecue on the edge of the beach, serving amazing freshly cooked fajitas – barbecued meat, onion, capsicum and chilli, served with tortillas and a scoop of black beans from a dubious plastic bucket.

When I awoke the next morning, I noticed two things: I had survived the mystery bucket of beans and a few of the people I had lined up with the night before were still enjoying the refreshing taste of the beer, although at that point I'm sure it didn't taste quite so fresh. Mexicans sure know how to party!

NATIONAL CHICKEN

MUST BE COOKED ON A HOODED BARBECUE*

PUT THE CHILLIES, GARLIC, SALT AND pepper in a pestle and mortar and pound into a paste. One by one add the oil, honey and lime zest and juice, pounding them into a paste. Stir in the coriander. You can also do this in a small food processor if you have one.

Put the chicken breast side down on a board and slice through the skin either side of the backbone. Then using poultry shears or sharp kitchen scissors cut either side of the back bone and remove. Turn the chicken over and press down firmly on the breast bone to flatten the chicken. Using scissors make a short cut through the skin at the neck to enable the chicken to sit completely flat. Using your fingers carefully loosen the skin from the breast flesh, being careful not to tear the skin. Spread half the chilli mixture under the skin, then rub the rest of the mixture all over the outside of the chicken. Set aside to marinate for a couple of hours if you have time. Remove from the fridge 20 minutes before cooking to return to room temperature.

It is preferable to cook the chicken on a flat plate (although the grill is also fine) and it must be dooked by indirect heat. If you have 3 or 4 burners, turn on the outside 2 only or if you only have 2 turn only one side on. Preheat barbecue to medium heat.

Put the chicken on the cooler part of the barbecue, breast side down. Cook for 10 minutes, rotating (not turning over) 2-3 times. Turn the chicken over and cook for a further 40-50 minutes, rotating 2-3 times. Check it is cooked by inserting a skewer into a thigh – the juices should run clear with no traces of blood, if there is any pink continue to cook. Remove from the heat, cover and leave for 10 minutes.

* If you don't have a hooded barbecue, make this with chicken pieces instead. Loosen the skin of each piece and spread with the mixture.

TOP TIP
A 2kg (5lb) chicken should feed about 6 people. A 1.6kg (3lb) chicken will feed about 4.

PREP: 30 minutes
COOK: about 1 hour
MAKES: 1 roast chicken

5 small red chillies, seeded and finely chopped
3 garlic cloves, crushed
½ teaspoon salt
Freshly ground black pepper
1 tablespoon olive oil
1 tablespoon honey
1 lime, finely grated zest and 1 tablespoon of juice
2 tablespoons chopped fresh coriander leaves
1 x 2kg (5 lb) chicken (see box)

ISLA MUJERES, MEXICO — ORANGE BARBECUE FISH

Roughly translated as 'Island of Women', this small island off the east coast of Mexico was the perfect place to lay back, relax and recover from the madness of the mainland.

I stumbled upon a large woodfire beachside barbecue and was informed that it was used as part of a half-day snorkelling tour with lunch provided - it seemed only fair that the fish had the chance to bite

me first, before I got the chance to bite back at lunch.

The tour guides prepared large mackerels marinated in orange mystery sauce and fresh lime juice, before cooking and smoking away on the barbecue within large metal grates. We ate the fish with our fingers, along with ice cold Coronas, fresh lime, and relaxing music in the background. Exactly what a Mexican barbecue is meant to be!

COW CUTS

The best bits for barbecuing from our cow mates are the rump, fillet and sirloin, all of which are found along the top of the beast – the area that does the least work. From here you get t-bone steaks, sirloin steaks, rump steaks, fillet steaks and porterhouse steaks. The shoulders and lower legs – which do the most work – are cheaper cuts. They have loads of flavour but they require longer cooking times.

NECK

RIB SET/
BEEF CUTLE

CHUCK

BLADE

BRISKET

SHORT RIBS

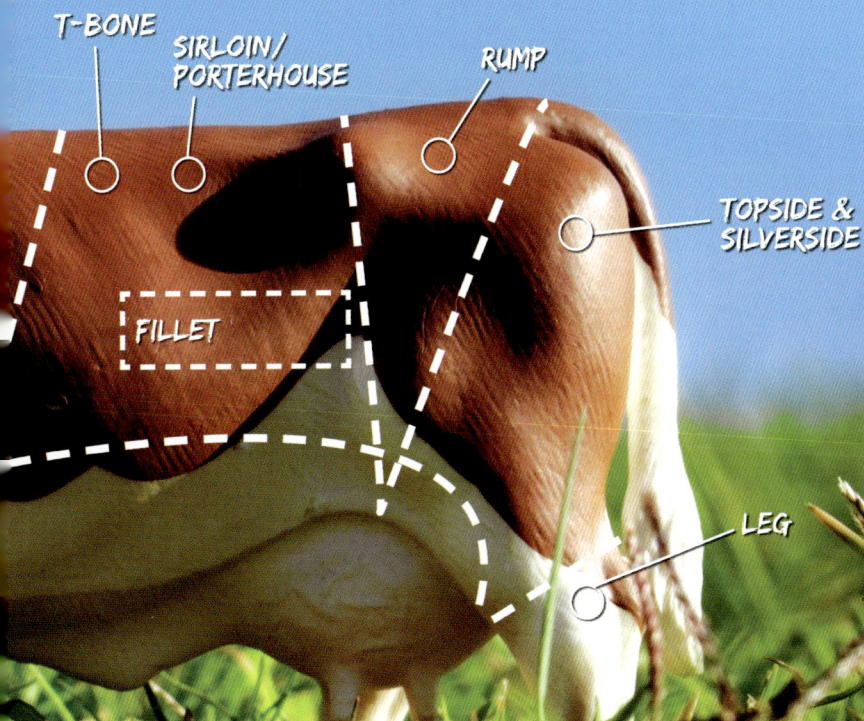

T-BONE

SIRLOIN/
PORTERHOUSE

RUMP

TOPSIDE &
SILVERSIDE

FILLET

LEG

FAJITAS

MORE A TEX-MEX DISH THAN strictly Mexican. Fajitas were invented by Mexican workers working in Texas. These can be as simple or as elaborate as you wish. There's no salsa included in this recipe, but feel free to buy a good quality salsa to serve with the fajitas, or use the one on page 86. If you don't have a flat plate on your barbecue, keep the meat whole, then slice before serving. You'll need to cook the meat for longer though.

Combine the meat, 2 tablespoons of olive oil and the red chillies in a bowl. Add plenty of freshly ground black pepper and mix. Set aside while you make everything else.

To make the guacamole, combine all the ingredients in a bowl, mixing gently. Put the sour cream (stirring quickly to soften) and grated cheese in separate small bowls. Wrap the tortillas in foil. Toss the capsicum and onion in the remaining oil.

Heat one barbecue flat plate to high and another either flat or grill plate to medium. Put the stack of foil-wrapped tortillas over the medium heat to warm through, turning the stack occasionally. Cook the meat over the high heat, turning regularly. If using chicken, cook for 5-6 minutes until cooked through. If using beef cook for about 3 minutes, as it can be served rare. Set aside in a warm place, then cook the capsicum and onion for 4-5 minutes until softened.

To assemble, spread a little sour cream on a tortilla, top with some meat and vegetables, grated cheese and a spoonful of guacamole. Roll up and eat immediately.

PREP: 30 minutes
COOK: about 10 minutes
MAKES: 8-10 tortillas

500g skirt or flank steak or skinless chicken breast, cut into thin strips
3 tablespoons olive oil
1-2 small red chillies, finely chopped
Black pepper
150g sour cream
100g grated cheese
2 red capsicums, cut into 1cm wide strips
1 red onion, halved, then cut into thin wedges
8-10 large flour tortillas

GUACAMOLE (OPTIONAL)
2 ripe avocados, cut into small cubes
3 tablespoons chopped fresh coriander
About 1 tablespoon lime juice

Feed me!

LIGHTING A CHARCOAL BARBECUE THE OSORNO VOLCANO WAY

Volcanos are capable of generating energy and heat in excess of hundreds of atomic bombs, which is an eye opening fact when you are standing at the base of one.

Volcan Osorno is situated south of Santiago in the lakes district of Chile. It's positioned on a lake's edge across from Puerto Varas, a friendly yet eerie little town often cloaked in fog and a somewhat mysterious force that had enticed me to stay longer – or perhaps it was just the scent of charcoal roasted beef, the warmed glass of red Chilean wine and friendly hospitality.

On the veranda of the hostel I was staying at, a local man named Pablo shared some invaluable charcoal barbecuing ingenuity. To my amazement, he demonstrated a five-step

fire lighting technique inspired by the volcano just behind us:

1. Position your barbecue away from strong winds and drafts.
2. Twist newspaper into rings gradually building them into the shape of a volcano, starting with a double layer of thickness on the lower levels.

3. Surround the outside of the paper with a stack of charcoal keeping a hole down the centre, allowing the fire to breath.
4. Light the paper at the base of your mini volcano.
5. Once the charcoal is fully alight, fold in the top of the charcoal to ensure an even spread of charcoal for cooking.

This approach ensures the oxygen required to burn the charcoal is available, but avoids problems of smouldering or the paper burning out before the charcoal is fully alight.

TIP Avoid the use of kerosene-infused charcoal which adds unwanted flavour beneath your food.

CAESAR SALAD

THIS UBIQUITOUS SALAD IS FOUND on menus the world over in various guises. It is most commonly believed to have been invented by Caesar Cardini an Italian-born-Mexican working in Mexico. To be truly authentic you could also assemble the salad in front of your guests as it is told that Mr Cardini himself did.

Put a baking tray (sheet) in the oven and preheat oven to 180°C (350°F/Gas 4). Meanwhile, wash the lettuce leaves, dry then put in a serving dish and chill in the fridge.

Cut the bread into 1cm squares and put into a bowl. Drizzle over 1 tablespoon of oil and toss well to evenly coat the bread. Spread the bread on the baking tray and bake for 5 minutes, shaking the tray occasionally, until the croutons are golden brown. Set aside to cool.

Squash the garlic halves with the side of a blunt knife, but don't crush completely. Put into the olive oil.

Put the egg in a heatproof bowl and pour boiling water into the bowl, not directly onto the egg as this could crack the shell. Leave for 10 minutes. Then remove the egg and run under cold water. Set aside.

When ready to serve, remove the garlic from the oil and put the oil, Worcestershire sauce, vinegar, lemon juice and black pepper in a medium bowl. Crack in the egg and whisk well. Toss the croutons into the lettuce leaves, drizzle over sufficient dressing to coat the salad and scatter over the Parmesan cheese. Serve immediately.

TOP TIP

This recipe contains raw egg. People with low immune systems should avoid eating raw egg, this includes pregnant women, the elderly and those with immune deficiency conditions.

PREP: 25 minutes
COOK: 5 minutes
SERVES: 6

3 medium Romaine lettuces, leaves separated
3 slices day-old crusty bread, crusts removed
125ml (½ cup) olive oil
1 garlic clove, halved
1 egg
Dash of Worcestershire sauce
1½ tablespoons white wine vinegar
Juice of 1 lemon
Freshly ground black pepper
30g freshly grated Parmesan cheese

DULCE DE LECHE

REMOVE ANY PAPER LABELS FROM the can and using a can opener pierce two small holes in the top on opposite sides of the can.

Sit the can in a saucepan and pour in water (bring careful not to splash the top) until it reaches 2.5cm from the top of the can. Bring to a simmer uncovered and once simmering turn down the heat, but you need to keep the water simmering. Simmer uncovered for about three hours for a soft textured dulce de leche and four hours for a firmer one. Top up the water as it evaporates and never let the pan boil dry or your can could explode.

Using tongs or an oven glove, remove the can from the pan and leave to cool on a wire rack. Once cool, wipe off any seepage on the top and open using a can opener. If cooking for only 3 hours you may find that the top is still runny. Simply pour and scoop it into a bowl and whisk to a smooth consistency. If cooked for 4 hours, it's still good to give it a quick whisk. Eat as is or serve on pancakes or with ice cream.

PREP: 2 minutes
COOK: 3-4 hours
SERVES: 6 (depending on size of your can)

400g can condensed milk

Please, don't eat me!

... take the beans instead

KEEPING FOOD FRESH – REAL WORLD FOOD SAFETY

A TRIP TO A MEXICAN FOOD MARKET, with meat hanging from the roof on big steel hooks for hours on end without a fridge in sight, provides a new perspective on food safety.

Having eaten endless amounts of kebabs, parrillas, churrascos and questionable snacks from restaurants and street-vendor barbecues, my experience demonstrates that we should be aware of food safety, but not scared about it.

To take the worry and stress out of cooking, follow these simple steps:

1 Take food out of the fridge shortly before cooking; leave just enough time for it to return to room temperature before cooking, but not longer than one hour sitting out of the fridge.
2 Wash your hands regularly.
3 Don't use utensils or plates from raw preparation to serve the cooked food.
4 Marinate food in the fridge.
5 Never use your marinade sauce as a dipping sauce later.
6 Food is better hot or cold, it's when it's warm that problems arise.
7 Defrost frozen food in the fridge if you have time – if not, use the microwave and cook immediately afterwards.
8 Don't put hot dishes directly into the fridge – the heat can affect other cold food.
9 Use paper towels – old kitchen dishcloths are a big offender for germs.
10 Pay special attention to chicken and wash down all surfaces afterwards.

MANGO AND TEQUILA SORBET

PUT THE SUGAR INTO A SMALL saucepan with 500ml (2 cups) water. Stir over low-medium heat until the sugar dissolves, do not allow to come to the boil. Once the sugar has dissolved bring to the boil, then reduce the heat and simmer for 5 minutes. Remove from the heat and leave to cool completely. Chill.

Meanwhile, whiz the mango flesh in a food processor until pureed. Add the cooled sugar syrup, tequila and lime zest and whiz again until thoroughly blended. Pour into a shallow metal tin (about 23cm square and at least 1.25L (5 cups) capacity) and freeze for 1½ hours or until almost frozen. Return to the blender and whiz again to break down any ice crystals. Return to the tin and freeze until sold.

To serve, working quickly as the sorbet will melt quickly, use a metal fork to break up the sorbet and serve in glasses.

TOP TIP
To cut the mango, sit the mango with the 2 fat sides crossways. Slice down either side of the stone. Then cut in a criss-cross shape through to the skin. Turn inside out then slice off the flesh. Remove as much flesh from around the stone as possible.

PREP: 35 minutes
SERVES: 6

230g (1 cup) caster (superfine) sugar
2 large, ripe mangoes, chopped (you need about 750g of flesh)
3 tablespoons (¼ cup) tequila
1 teaspoon finely grated lime zest

OK, just one more parrilla

It's not Wagyu

BOLIVIAN SALT FLATS

Besides good barbecue fuel and high quality meat, I've always felt that salt is the next most important element in barbecuing.

After leaving Argentina, I decided to further indulge my fascination with salt by visiting the world's largest salt flats. These are located in southwestern Bolivia near the small town of Salar de Uyuni, where travellers begin their tour of the salt flats in beaten-up 4WDs.

Prior to visiting Salar de Uyuni, I had only ever experienced salt in salt shakers, or coating a piece of meat. When it covers the entire surface of the earth around you, it assaults your senses. The sun reflects off the salty surface deep into your retinas and, with no obstacles in its path, the wind tears through your entire body. Was this revenge for all the salt I've used during barbecuing over the years?

On a positive note, it creates a brilliant opportunity to belittle your mates when you begin to lose perspective and the salt plays tricks on your eyes as there are no landmarks to judge distance or scale.

TORRES DEL PAINE, PATAGONIA – TOO SORE TO BARBECUE

THE OLD SAYING 'THERE'S NO pleasure without pain' has never been as true as in Torres Del Paine National Park in southern Chile. It should simply be spelt Torres Del PAIN!

The Patagonian region provides the most gruelling yet beautiful hiking and barbecue backdrop in the world – yes, I know it's a big call! The scenery includes green paddocks with wild, ice-frosted horses, jagged snow-capped mountains, and bobbing icebergs escaping the spectacular Grey Glacier that shone aqua blue in the sunlight.

Leading into the four day, 75 km trek, my excitement was weighed down by my portable barbecue and carbohydrate-loaded backpack. On arrival at the nightly Refugio accommodation, my starved body screamed for carbohydrates to replace those stripped from aching muscles during the day's walk. It was time to eat.

I wish I could tell you about the most scenic barbecue of my life, but it would be a lie. My grand plans had been replaced by gale-force winds, -12^{0}C temperatures and sore muscles. My barbecue remained in my backpack, while I sat near the heater, eating from a tin of cold beans.

On the last day, as we geared up to walk back to the national park gateway, a mammoth 20 km away, I imagined sitting in the back of my own backpack, legs hanging, as I'm carried out by my friends. Fortunately my aching legs lasted the journey and I was saved the embarrassment – real men don't ride in backpacks!

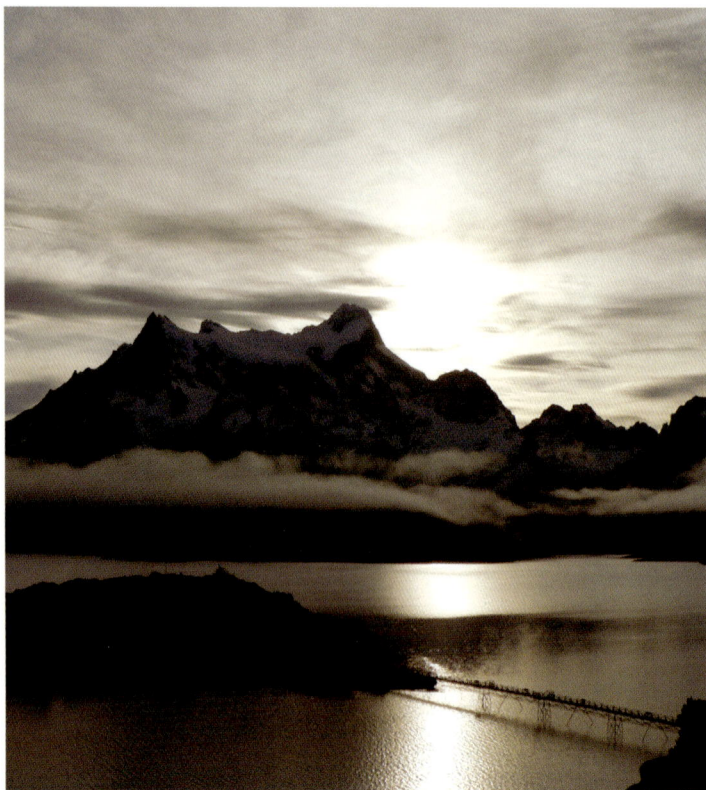

Has the author found the ultimate barbie spot?

MENDOZA, ARGENTINA – WINE & RIBS

IT SEEMS ONLY FAIR THAT ARGENTINA, the red meat capital of South America, has its own red wine region. Inland from Santiago, cool climates, pure Andean waters and some of the highest altitudes in the world for growing grapes provide the perfect conditions for producing these renowned Malbec wines. Fine restaurants around the world are using food and alcohol matching to enhance the dining experience, and barbecuing is no different. I spent three nights eating at the same parrilla restaurant, trialling new Malbecs with barbecue ribs – yes, I ate ribs three nights in a row. Now it's hard for me to imagine Argentinean ribs (asado de tira) without a silky glass of Malbec from Mendoza.

THE LARES VALLEY TREK

After a few days acclimatising in Cuzco, i.e. drinking and partying into the early hours, the Lares Trek began. It was a 4-day walk across high mountain peaks that literally took my breath away, before crossing valleys with ancient Incan villages on our way to Machu Picchu.

On the second night, I was invited to attend an evening barbecue at a local village. I soon received hints to the menu for the evening when a man pointed at the guinea pigs scattered around the dark floor of the mud brick house and said, with a cheeky smile: 'No es pets'. It added new meaning to 'watch what you eat!'

The guinea pigs were butterflied and cooked over an open fire. Having moved past the fact that I had just eaten one of my childhood pets, the meat itself was quite tender and enjoyable. I would, however, advise if you are planning on trying either guinea pigs or alpaca in Peru to do so in Cuzco before you become too attached to them during your trek.

ASIA

IN ASIA, BARBECUING RELIES ON the fusion of food flavours and an adventurous approach to food that's not only tasty but is also an interactive and entertaining experience.

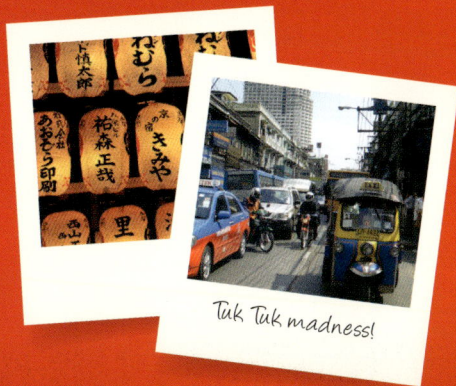

Tuk Tuk madness!

BARBECUED THAI FISHCAKES

THESE ARE NORMALLY SHALLOW fried but they can just as easily be made on the barbecue. The only trouble is, as fast as you cook them, people will eat them! They can be made in advance and refrigerated until you are ready to cook them.

Make sure any skin and bones are removed from the fish, then roughly chop. Put the fish into a food processor and process for about 20 seconds until smooth. Add the curry paste, chilli, egg, fish sauce, lime leaves and coriander leaves and blend for about 10 seconds. Transfer to a mixing bowl and stir in the beans.

Using slightly wet hands take heaped tablespoons of the mixture and shape into flattish cakes about 5cm across, you should be making about 15. Get the flat plate (or grill if you don't have one) of your barbecue hot and pour on a good layer of oil. Cook the fish cakes in a single layer for 3-4 minutes on each side, until golden brown, ensuring they are cooked all the way through. Drain on paper towel then serve immediately accompanied by bowls of sweet chilli sauce for dipping.

TOP TIP

You really need a food processor to make these as the mixture needs to be all blended together. If you don't have one and you really want to make them, then very finely chop everything, then mix well together.

PREP: 40 minutes
COOK: about 8 minutes
MAKES: about 15 small fish cakes

450g firm white fish fillets
1 tablespoon red curry paste
1 green chilli, seeded and finely chopped
1 egg, lightly beaten
1 tablespoon fish sauce
4 kaffir lime leaves, finely shredded
3 tablespoons chopped fresh coriander
  leaves
50g green beans, finely sliced
vegetable oil, for frying
Sweet chilli sauce, to serve

BARBECUEASIA

Walking through an Asian food market is a truly eye-opening experience. In stark contrast to the fluorescent lights and organisation of Western supermarkets, these markets are gastronomic chaos at its best. Fresh, lively and at times weird looking seafood, meat and produce, are the starting points for many great barbecues across Asia.

My Asian barbecue adventure began in Singapore, self-proclaimed food capital of Asia. Singapore is renowned for chilli and black pepper crab and satays of all descriptions. Hawker food in Singapore are as good as I've found anywhere in the world.

With high expectations I moved on from the food capital to the food giant of Asia – China. With over 1.3 billion hungry mouths to feed, China has no choice but to focus on food.

After the initial confusion about where to start looking for China's contribution to barbecuing, standout dishes soon appeared. Like the Great Wall of China, when something is so spectacular, it's impossible to keep it hidden for long. I'm referring to Szechuan cuisine and Peking duck.

Asia has an amazing range of chilli dips and condiments that often accompany meals, but Szechuan takes things to a new level. It's a spicy style of cooking and was the source of the hottest barbecue I've ever tasted, perhaps only matched by a habanero barbecue dipping sauce in Mexico, which even a couple icy cold Coronas couldn't fix.

Finding good Peking duck wasn't as tough on my taste buds. I visited many great restaurants, and discovered each provided an enticing range of smoky wood-fired flavours. And, in line with most great barbecues, each was accompanied by its own style of barbecue sauce. I now hold Peking duck in high esteem next to Argentinean ribs and US pulled pork. For food lovers it's up there with the Great Wall of China as an essential Asian experience.

TIP: In many parts of Asia, red meat is scarcity or poor quality. Anything reasonabe is often imported or very expensive, so it's worth taking the lead of the locals by sticking to seafood, chicken and pork, served along with vegetables and rice of course. It's also a reminder that when you get the chance to try high quality beef, you've got to go for it.

SAKE CLAMS

CALLED "ASARI NO SAKAMUSHI" IN Japan, this is a recipe for steaming clams in sake. Asari clams are 2-3cm across, so look for ones about this size, if you can't get them don't worry use what you can get.

Give the clams a quick scrub. Put in a bowl of water and leave to soak in the fridge overnight or for several hours. This helps to remove grit and sand.

Discard any clams that aren't closed or which don't close when tapped with a knife. Drain in a colander.

Cut four pieces of aluminium foil about 25 x 30cm. Put eight clams in two rows of four in the middle of each piece of foil. Neatly fold in the sides, add about 1 tablespoon of sake to each parcel then fold in one end. Fold in the second end folding it over the first end to form a neat, tight, sealed parcel. Ensure there are no holes in your parcels, if there are make a new one otherwise all the sake will leak out.

Preheat barbecue to high. Put the parcels on the heat and leave for 4-6 minutes or until the parcels pop open. With less powerful barbecues it is possible the parcels won't pop, so after 4 minutes open a parcel to see if the clams have opened, if so remove the parcel. Once the parcels or clams have opened remove from the heat. Sit each foil parcel in a small bowl and serve from the foil. Serve immediately. Eat with small forks. Do not eat any clams that do not open.

PREP: 10 minutes (plus overnight soaking)
COOK: 4-5 minutes
SERVES: 4

About 32 clams
4 tablespoons sake

TOP TIP
This is also delicious served as a pasta entrée. Cook some angel hair pasta and toss the clams and the cooking liquid through with plenty of black pepper and a tablespoon of chopped flat leaf parsley.

My mouth's watering already

So that's what the wok's for

BANANA LEAF RED SNAPPER

2 BEER RATING

BANANA LEAVES CAN SOMETIMES be tough, so to soften and make them easier to handle, bring a large saucepan of water to the boil and put the leaves in for 1 minute then refresh under cold water. Take 2 of the leaves and put one on top of the other, so they overlap by about 10cm, thus making one longer leaf. Repeat with the other 2 leaves on top to create a double layer, repeat with the other 4 leaves so you have 2 sets of leaves.

Cut 3 diagonal slices across each side of the fish. Combine the coconut milk and curry paste. Brush about 2 tablespoons onto one side of each fish then lay one fish coconut milk side down onto each leaf. Spoon about 2 tablespoons into the cavity of each fish, then brush the remaining mixture on top of the fish. Tear up two of the lime leaves and put inside the cavities with the squashed lemongrass. Scatter the sliced chilli on top of the fish and then arrange the whole lime leaves on top.

Wrap the fish in the leaf, securing with several toothpicks.

Preheat barbecue to medium-low. Cook the fish for 10 minutes, spraying or brushing regularly with water then turn over and cook for a further 10 minutes or until the fish flakes easily with a fork. The leaves may burn, but this shouldn't matter. Unwrap at the table to allow the delicious aromas to escape. Scatter over the coriander leaves and serve.

TOP TIP
Banana leaves are usually available in Asian supermarkets or from the banana tree in your garden! If you can't find them then you can use foil instead.

PREP: 25 minutes
COOK: about 25 minutes
MAKES: 2 whole fish, serves 4-6

8 banana leaves, each measuring about 60cm long (see box)
2 x 1kg whole red snapper or bream, scaled, fins removed and gutted
200ml coconut milk
½-1 tablespoon green curry paste
8 kaffir lime leaves
3 red chillies, sliced on the diagonal
2 lemon grass stalks, halved and squashed
Handful fresh coriander leaves, to serve
Toothpicks

Man, it's humid!

Saving some for later

DRY CHILLI CHICKEN

THIS MUST BE COOKED ON THE FLAT plate of a barbecue as it is quite saucy. If you don't have one, put a large flat chargrill pan or frying pan onto the barbecue and heat it well before cooking the chicken.

Whisk together the light soy sauce, sugar, black pepper, sesame oil and egg white. Put the chicken in a medium bowl, pour over the marinade and leave to marinate for 30 minutes. Meanwhile, prepare the vegetables and combine the sauce ingredients.

Oil the flat plate of your barbecue (you can't use a grill) and get it hot. Drain the liquid from the chicken and fry the chicken on the flat plate for about 2 minutes until golden, turning it regularly. Remove from the barbecue.

Add sufficient vegetable oil to the hot plate to coat it. Add the chillies and cook for 30 seconds. Add the onion and capsicum and cook for 1 minute. Add the chicken and the sauce and cook for about 1 minute, stirring regularly until most of the sauce has evaporated and it's all a bit sticky. Serve immediately being careful of the vast number of chillies! Serve with rice or bread.

PREP: 30 minutes
COOK: 5 minutes
SERVES: 4

1 tablespoon light soy sauce
1 tablespoon sugar
½ teaspoon black pepper
2 teaspoons sesame oil
1 egg white, whisked until frothy
500g skinless chicken breast, thinly sliced
10 dried red chillies, halved lengthways and seeded
1 onion, halved and cut into thin wedges
1 green capsicum, deseeded and cut into 2cm wide slices
2 tablespoons vegetable oil
Rice or bread to serve

SAUCE:
1 tablespoon honey
1 tablespoon oyster sauce
1 tablespoon light soy sauce
½ teaspoon sugar
1 teaspoon sesame oil
Salt and black pepper

SATAY CLUB, SINGAPORE

Recommended by a Singaporean colleague, I followed the mouth-watering scent of sizzling satays towards the open air dining of the Satay Club. I couldn't help but wonder how this would compare to the high expectations that had been set by the Singaporean chilli and black pepper crabs I'd eaten the night before.

Upon arrival, I watched street vendors busily attending their barbecues to ensure a constant flow of delicious satay skewers to passers-by. There was a buzz in the air as the friendly yet persistent vendors promoted their satay delights whilst the humidity promoted consumption of the beer. At the end of the night, a pile of empty skewers gave testament to the uniquely Singaporean barbecue experience of the Satay Club.

LANGKAWI, MALAYSIA — THE ONE THAT GOT AWAY

Not all barbecues turn out the way you plan. I arrived at a beachside restaurant that proudly showcased some of the freshest seafood I had ever seen, along with the scent of a newly lit charcoal barbecue.

Overwhelmed by excitement and the extremely low prices, I pointed out the biggest lobster I could find. As I patiently waited for the lobster to cook, I realised it wasn't just my mouth that was watering. My whole body began to sweat and the room began to spin. Perhaps the seafood entree from the makeshift beachside grill on the way to dinner wasn't such a great idea. I fought off the ill feelings just long enough to see the lobster arrive on the table, before embarrassingly running out of the restaurant without a single bite. I still wonder today how it would have tasted and hope that one of the restaurant staff were able to enjoy one of the few barbecue meals I've ever turned away!

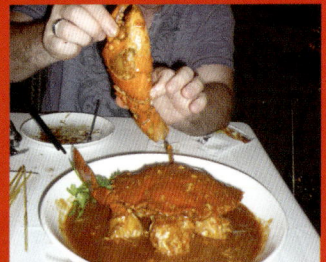

GRILLED VIETNAMESE PORK MEAT-BALLS WITH NUOC MAM CHAM SAUCE

2 BEER RATING

TO MAKE THE MEATBALLS, PUT THE pork mince in a large bowl and mash briefly with your hands. Add the remaining ingredients and mix until well combined. Take tablespoons of the mixture and form into 18 balls. Thread 3 balls onto each skewer. Chill for an hour or so in the fridge.

To make the nuoc mam cham sauce, dissolve the sugar in half the fish sauce. Add the remaining fish sauce, chilli, lime juice and 1 tablespoon of water.

Preheat barbecue to medium-hot. Grill the meatballs for about 6 minutes turning once or twice, or until cooked through but not dry. Serve immediately accompanied by the dipping sauce.

If preferred, the meatballs can be served individually. If using long metal skewers put several on and barbecue. Once cooked, remove from the skewers, put into a serving dish and serve accompanied by the dipping sauce.

PREP: 45 minutes
COOK: about 8 minutes
SERVES: 4-6 (makes 18 small meatballs)

MEATBALLS:
500g pork mince (not too lean)
1 tablespoon sugar
1 red chilli, finely chopped
7cm lemongrass stalk, finely chopped
3 garlic cloves, crushed
2 tablespoons fish sauce
2 tablespoons finely chopped mint leaves
2 tablespoons finely chopped coriander leaves
Salt and freshly ground black pepper
6 metal or wooden skewers

NUOC MAM CHAM SAUCE:
(Vietnamese dipping sauce with lime)
1 teaspoon sugar
2 tablespoons fish sauce
1 red chilli, finely chopped
1½ tablespoons lime juice

If using wooden skewers soak them in water while making the meatballs.

MARKET CREATURES

With a flash of fire from a wok, I stook mesmerised by street vendors juggling exotic creatures and a colourful list of ingredients, from ginger, chilli and garlic to lime leaves, coconut and shrimp paste. At this point, I couldn't help but wonder if woks were a barbecue creation designed to stop the lively market creatures from escaping, or if the deep pans were simply a reflection of the depth of flavours and complexity within Asian cooking.

INTERACTIVE BARBECUE EXPERIENCE

Asia provides a barbecue experience that not only tastes great, but that entertains. A uniquely interactive style of cooking distracts you as you wait for the food to be prepared. In Tokyo, be entertained as you eat food flying directly from the hot plates at a tepanyaki restaurant, enjoy the scent of Korean barbecue delights cooked at your table, or be amazed by Thai street vendors who make irresistible banana pancakes in beachside huts.

Just remember: egg on your face at a tepanyaki, or banana down your shirt after being distracted by a Thai street vendors is all part of the barbecue experience.

SINGAPORE SATAY CHICKEN

SLICE THE CHICKEN LENGTHWAYS into 1cm wide slices. Combine the coriander, turmeric, chilli powder, garlic, oyster sauce, lemon grass and soy sauce with 2 tablespoons of water. Put the chicken in a non-metallic dish and pour the marinade over, mix well. Refrigerate for at least 2 hours and up to 24 hours.

To make the sauce, heat the oil in a small saucepan over low-medium heat. Add the curry paste and fry gently, stirring regularly for 2 minutes until it smells really fragrant. Add the peanut butter, soy sauce and coconut milk and cook for 1–2 minutes, stirring until smooth. Transfer to a serving dish and leave to cool to room temperature.

While cooling, put a piece of plastic wrap on the surface of the sauce to prevent a skin forming.

Soak skewers in water for at least 20 minutes, to stop them burning.

Remove the chicken from the fridge 20 minutes before cooking to return to room temperature. Thread the chicken onto the skewers, putting just 1 or 2 pieces onto each skewer.

Preheat barbecue to medium. Cook the chicken for 5-7 minutes until just cooked through, turning regularly, until golden all over. Do not overcook or it will be dry. Serve the sauce along-side the chicken skewers.

PREP: 30 minutes
COOK: about 10 minutes
MAKES: about 16 skewers

500g skinless chicken breasts
1 teaspoon ground coriander
1 teaspoon ground turmeric
1 teaspoon chilli powder
1 garlic clove, crushed
1 tablespoon oyster sauce
½ lemon grass stalk, finely chopped
1 tablespoon soy sauce
16 wooden skewers

SATAY SAUCE:
2 teaspoons vegetable oil
2 teaspoons red curry paste
100g crunchy peanut butter
1 tablespoon soy sauce
165ml can coconut milk

KOREAN BEEF

TO MAKE SLICING THE BEEF EASIER, put it in the freezer for 30 minutes before slicing (do this while you make the marinade). Once frozen, use a very sharp knife to slice across the beef into thin slices about 5mm (½ cm) thick. Put into a shallow dish.

To make the marinade, peel, core and puree or mush up the nashi pear, or peel and puree or mush up the kiwi. Put in a bowl with the remaining ingredients and plenty of black pepper and stir until the honey and sugar are dissolved and well mixed. (This can all be done in a blender if you have one.) Pour over the beef, mix well and leave for at least 1 hour and up to 3 hours.

Wash the lettuce leaves and pat dry. Put in a serving bowl and refrigerate until needed.

Preheat barbecue grill plate to high. Remove the beef from the marinade and pat dry. Grill the beef in a single layer for about 1 minute, turn over and cook for 20-30 seconds. The meat is very delicate so take care when cook-ing it. Serve immediately, accompa-nied by the lettuce leaves.

To serve put 1 or 2 pieces of beef in a lettuce leaf and wrap up. If serving rice with this, place a small amount inside the lettuce with the beef and wrap up.

PREP: 30 minutes (+ 30 minutes freezing)
COOK: 2 minutes
SERVES: 4

600g piece sirloin beef (it needs to be a
    thick piece)
1 soft lettuce, leaves separated
Steamed or boiled rice, to serve (optional)

MARINADE:
1 ripe nashi pear or kiwi
3 garlic cloves, crushed
60ml (¼ cup) soy sauce
1 tablespoon honey
2 tablespoons brown sugar
1 tablespoon mirin (Japanese rice wine)
2 teaspoons sesame oil
Freshly ground black pepper

JAPANESE CHARGRILLED TUNA SALAD WITH SESAME DRESSING

COMBINE ALL THE DRESSING ingredients in a small bowl. Put the salad leaves in a serving dish. Cut the onions into 5cm lengths, then slice very thinly lengthways. Set aside.

Preheat the grill plate of your barbecue to hot. Brush each tuna steak with olive oil and season with salt and freshly ground black pepper. Cook on a hot barbecue for 3 minutes on one side then turn over and cook for a further 3 minutes, the fish should have good stripes on the outside and still be pink in the middle. The cooking time will depend on the thickness of your fish, do not overcook.

Sit the fish for a couple of minutes, then slice thinly. Toss half the salad dressing over the leaves. Arrange the sliced fish on top of the salad leaves, scatter the onions over the top and drizzle over the remaining dressing.

Asian barbecue surprise!

PREP: 10 minutes
COOK: about 6 minutes
SERVES: 4

150g mixed lettuce leaves
3 salad onions (spring onions/green shallots)
4 x 150-180g tuna steaks
Olive oil, for brushing
Salt and black pepper

DRESSING:
2 tablespoons vegetable oil
2 tablespoons Japanese rice vinegar
2 teaspoons mirin (Japanese rice wine)
1 teaspoon light soy sauce
1 teaspoon sugar
½ teaspoon sesame oil
1 teaspoon toasted sesame seeds

TERIYAKI CHICKEN

IF USING WOODEN SKEWERS, SOAK them in water for an hour to prevent them burning on the barbecue.

Put all the ingredients, except the chicken in a small saucepan. Bring to the boil, then reduce the heat and simmer for 10 minutes until the sauce has thickened slightly. Remove from the heat and cool.

Put the chicken in a bowl and pour the sauce over. Leave to marinate for at least an hour and up to 24 hours.

Remove from the fridge about 20 minutes before cooking to allow to come to room temperature.

Skewer the chicken about 6 pieces per skewer.

Heat your barbecue to medium heat. Cook the kebabs for 12-15 minutes, turning regularly. Do not cook them too fast otherwise the outside will burn and the inside will be raw. Be careful not to overcook them or they will dry out.

PREP: 25 minutes
COOK: 25 minutes
SERVES: 8 kebabs

125ml (1/2 cup) soy sauce
80ml (1/3 cup) sake
80ml (1/3 cup) mirin (Japanese rice wine)
1 tablespoon sugar
1 tablespoon grated ginger
750g skinless, chicken breasts, cut into 2cm cubes
8 wooden or metal skewers

WAGYU BEEF

WAGYU BEEF IS THE LEGENDARY beef of Japan, originally from Kobe. Although originally from Japan it is now available outside of Japan and if you're lucky enough to find some you should give it a go. It's imperative that you don't overcook the meat or you will have wasted your money. If you can't get wagyu, sirloin steak is fine to use instead.

Combine the dipping sauce ingredients and put into a couple of small serving dishes.

Brush the beef on both sides with oil and season with black pepper.

Half the pumpkin wedge crossways and then carefully slice lengthways into thin slices, leaving the skin on. Put into a bowl with the mushrooms and leeks. Drizzle over a tablespoon or so of oil, add plenty of salt and pepper and toss everything together well.

Preheat you barbecue to hot. Put the pumpkin on the barbecue, followed by the mushrooms and leeks and cook for a couple of minutes on each side, or until they are all tender, remove the vegetables as they are cooked. Transfer to a serving plate and keep warm. Now cook the beef. Sear the slices in a single layer for about 30 seconds then turn over and cook for a further ½-1 minute, although this will depend on the heat of your barbecue. You want the meat to be seared on the outside and rare in the middle, so don't overcook.

Serve immediately accompanied by the vegetables and dipping sauce.

SLICING YOUR MEAT

Wagyu needs to be sliced horizontally, with the grain, otherwise it will be chewy. It's best to ask your butcher to do this when you buy it, so request it sliced horizontally into slices about 5mm thick. Some butchers may not be able to do this, so if you need to do this yourself, freeze the meat for about 30 minutes, then use a very sharp knife to slice it. To make it easier you can cut it across into 2 pieces first.

TOP TIP

If you ever get the chance to cook a whole steak it's important to cook it correctly or you will spoil it. You must get your barbie hot before you start cooking. It should be crispy and seared on the outside, but still very rare in the middle. If you over cook it YOU WILL RUIN IT. Do NOT cook it so the fat starts to melt, otherwise you will end up with a tough, dry piece of meat.

The intense marbling of the meat is its joy!

PREP: 15 minutes
COOK: 10 minutes
SERVES: 4 when served alongside other dishes

400g wagyu beef or sirloin steak, sliced (see box)
2 tablespoons olive oil
Black pepper and salt
250g wedge of pumpkin, skin on
8 fresh shiitaki mushrooms
4 baby leeks or fat spring onions, trimmed and cut into 8cm lengths

PONZU DIPPING SAUCE:
2 tablespoons grapefruit or lime juice
2 tablespoons rice vinegar
1½ tablespoons soy sauce
1½ tablespoons mirin (Japanese rice wine)
Freshly ground black pepper

SOY AND GINGER BARBECUED FISH

WASH THE FISH INSIDE AND OUT and pat dry with paper towel. Make 3 cuts across each side of the fish and arrange in a single layer in a shallow dish or two. Combine the marinade ingredients and pour over the fish, spooning a little inside each fish too. Cover and leave to marinate for 1 hour, turning the fish once after half an hour.

Preheat barbecue to medium-hot. Remove the fish from the marinade and pat dry. Grill the fish for 3-4 minutes then carefully turn over. Grill for a further 3-4 minutes or until the fish is cooked and it flakes easily with a fork. Scatter the shredded spring onions and coriander over the top to serve. Serve with rice and salad or vegetables.

TOP TIP

Mirin is used predominantly in Japanese cooking. It is quite sweet as it has a high sugar content. Track it down in Japanese supermarkets or in the speciality aisles of some supermarkets. Use the rest of the bottle in other marinades, salad dressing or stews, just fling in a bit whenever a bit of sweetness is required, it's great stuff. If you can't get it then you could replace it with sweet sherry but the flavour will be quite different.

PREP: 15 minutes
COOK: 6-8 minutes
SERVES: 4

4 small whole fish (weighing about 300g each), such as bream, red mullet or rainbow trout, scaled and cleaned
3 salad onions (spring onions/green shallots)
2 tablespoons chopped fresh coriander leaves

MARINADE:
3 tablespoons (¼ cup) soy sauce
1 teaspoon sesame oil
2 tablespoons mirin (see box)
5cm piece fresh ginger, grated
1 small red chilli, deseeded and finely chopped (optional)

JAPANESE MISO FISH

LOOK FOR MIRIN AND WHITE MISO paste in Asian supermarkets and store the miso in the fridge once opened. This is a very popular dish in Japanese homes and restaurants.

Put the sake and mirin in a small saucepan and bring to the boil. Reduce heat to medium and add the miso, whisking until it dissolves. Add the sugar and stir until it dissolves. Set aside to cool. Put the fish in a shallow dish and pour over the cooled marinade. Cover and leave to marinate for at least 4 hours, but preferably overnight.

Remove from the fridge, allow to come to room temperature. Preheat barbecue flat plate or grill to hot. Scrape off the marinade and cook for about 3 minutes on each side, depending on the thickness of your fish. Set aside to rest for 5 minutes, then serve accompanied by the pickled ginger. Served with steamed rice, and a simple salad or green vegetable.

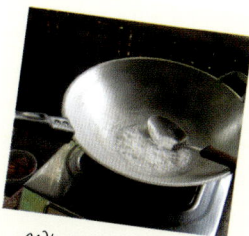

Who knows what's cooking this time!

PREP: 10 minutes
COOK: 8 minutes
SERVES: 4

80ml (1/3 cup) sake
80ml (1/3 cup) mirin (Japanese rice wine)
4 tablespoons (80g) white miso paste
3 tablespoons (45g) white sugar
4 x 180g skinless salmon, trout or cod fillets
Oil
Good quality pickled ginger, for serving (optional)

BANANA AND CHOCOLATE PANCAKES

MELT HALF THE BUTTER AND LEAVE to cool slightly. Put the flour, sugar and baking powder in a bowl and mix briefly. Add the eggs, honey and milk and whisk (with a hand whisk or electric beaters) until smooth. Slowly whisk in the melted butter. Set aside for 30 minutes.

Add the mashed banana to the pancake batter. Heat your (cleaned!) barbecue flat plate to medium-hot or line your plate with a liner. Reduce heat to low when you start cooking. Put a little butter on the flat plate and once melted spoon a heaped table-spoonful of batter onto the flat plate, and spread into a circle about 10cm (4in) across. Cook for about 1 minute until air bubbles start to form on the surface. Carefully turn the pancake over and cook the other side for about 30 seconds or until just golden. Repeat with the remaining mixture, adding more butter as necessary, cooking as many as you can at a time without them touching. The first few may not be perfect, it's a bit of trial and error to get the temperature right. Keep the cooked ones warm while you cook the rest. Serve immediately with some chocolate sauce drizzled over.

PREP: 20 minutes
COOK: about 15 minutes
SERVES: about 15 pancakes

Before you start making these give the flat plate of your barbecue a very good scrub, otherwise your pancakes could taste of sausages, steak and chicken! You can of course cook these in a frying pan instead.

50g butter
100g plain flour (or 50:50 plain and whole-meal flour)
25g caster sugar
1 tablespoon baking powder
2 eggs, lightly beaten
2 tablespoons honey
125ml (½ cup) semi-skimmed milk
3 bananas, well mashed
Good quality chocolate sauce, to serve

Another day, another rice paddy

Top-up?

MIDDLE EAST

THE MIDDLE EAST HAS A
community orientated and open
door approach to barbecues, with
religious holidays and family events
creating joyous occasions to be shared
between family and friends.

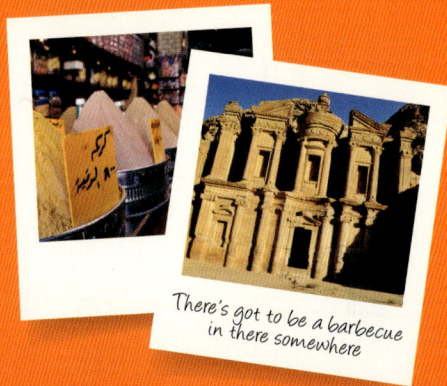

There's got to be a barbecue
in there somewhere

HAND GRENADES

TO MAKE THE FILLING, HEAT A LARGE frying pan over medium heat. Put the pine nuts in the pan and dry fry for 1 minute until golden. Remove from the pan. Add the oil to the pan and once it is hot, add the onion and fry for about 5 minutes until golden, stirring regularly. Add the mince and fry until browned. Stir in the pine nuts, season with salt and pepper and mix well. Remove from the heat and leave to cool slightly.

To make the shell, soak the burghul in water for 30 minutes. Put the meat in a food processor and process to a paste. Transfer to a large bowl. Put the onion, mint, basil and chilli (if using) in the processor and process to a paste. Add to the meat paste. Drain the burghul squeezing out any excess water. Add to the meat paste, season well with salt and pepper and mix everything together very well, working it through with your hands for 4-5 minutes, adding a little bit of water to moisten the mixture, if needed.

Wet your hands with cold water, then take a lump of mixture about the size of an egg and mould into the shape of a hand grenade. Using your finger, make a hole down the center of the hand grenade big enough to add about one tablespoon of filling. Turning the hand grenade in your hand use your fingers to carefully hollow out the hole. (The outside layer should be about 1 cm thick.) Add 1 tablespoon of the filling, then wet the rim with cold water and seal up. If any holes appear in the outer shell, wet your finger and use to seal the hole. Reshape if necessary, and set aside.

Preheat barbecue to medium with the hood down if you have one. Put a tablespoon of oil in a bowl, put each grenade in the bowl and coat lightly in oil. Grill with the hood down for about 6 minutes, turning once. If you don't have a hood you may need to cook them for a little longer. Serve with your choice of accompaniments.

PREP: 1½ hours
COOK: 6 minutes
MAKES: about 14 hand grenades

FILLING:
40g (1/3 cup) pine nuts
1 tablespoon olive oil, plus extra for brushing
1 medium onion, finely chopped
180g lamb or beef mince
Salt and pepper

SHELL:
250g (1¼ cups) fine burghul (crushed wheat)
500g lamb or beef mince
1 large onion, finely chopped
2 tablespoons chopped fresh mint leaves
2 tablespoons chopped fresh basil leaves (optional)
1 red chilli, seeded and chopped (optional)
Salt and Pepper

TO SERVE: (OPTIONAL)
Toasted pitta bread
Tomato and onion salad (from Turkish lamb kebabs, page 68)
Plain yoghurt with diced cucumber stirred in

HUMMUS

DRAIN THE SOAKED CHICKPEAS. PUT into a large saucepan and cover with plenty of water to cover by about 5cm (do not add salt). Bring to the boil, then reduce the heat and simmer for 45-50 minutes, until very soft (this could even take an hour), skimming off any scum. Drain, reserving the cooking liquid, then leave to cool for 20 minutes. Remove any loose skins.

Put the chickpeas in a food processor. Add the tahini, garlic and salt and process briefly. With the motor running gradually add the lemon juice and sufficient reserved cooking water to form a smooth creamy puree. Transfer to a flat serving dish. Whisk the paprika into the oil and drizzle over the humus. Scatter the parsley over the top and serve. If making in advance, leave in the food processor and give a final whiz before serving, adding a bit more water if needed.

Serve with toasted pitta bread or pide. Delicious served with the kofta on p137.

PREP: 20 minutes (plus overnight soaking)
COOK: 45-50 minutes
SERVES: 8

200g dried chickpeas, washed and soaked overnight
4 tablespoons (1/3 cup) tahini
1 large garlic clove, crushed
1 teaspoon salt
100ml lemon juice (2-3 lemons)
Pinch paprika (optional)
Olive oil, to drizzle
1 tablespoon chopped fresh parsley, to garnish
Toasted pitta bread or pide to serve

MID-EAST FEASTS

Don't be tempted to grab a quick snack before a Middle Eastern barbecue. The generous and hospitable nature of these family-orientated social gatherings will ensure you walk, or should I say roll, home with your pant's button undone, due to your bulging stomach and the words 'Bah, you've hardly eaten anything, have another plate' ringing in your ears.

Often overshadowed by its turbulent recent past, the Middle East offers some of the world's best cuisines, spectacular scenery and a barbecue social scene that rivals anywhere in the world.

Barbecues are often enjoyed on weekends, at family celebrations and around the various Christian, Jewish and Muslim religious holidays. For the bigger occasions such as births, deaths and marriages it's not uncommon to see a lamb, goat or other animal sacrificed and barbecued for family, friends and the wider community.

Due to the importance of these occasions, barbecue attire is often more formal than other parts of the world, but don't be fooled: it doesn't mean the locals won't let loose with laughter, singing, and dancing until late into the night.

The generally warm climate and an emphasis on social gatherings dictate that the barbecue food needs to incorporate small mezze plates, similar to tapas. Its staples include flat/pita breads, dips, skewered meats, seafood, lentils, salads, fresh fruit and nuts and a range of herbs and spices.

Religion also influences the type of foods at Middle Eastern barbecues. Kosher and halal meats need to be slaughtered and prepared in specific ways before they can be enjoyed. Religion can also exclude alcohol and certain types of meat such as pork.

Lebanon offers some of the regions most popular food. This small country with contrasting landscapes means that within 45 minutes you can be swimming at the beach or skiing snowy slopes, with scenic vineyards and fruit plantations in between.

Invited or not, when you arrive at a Lebanese barbecue, you feel like you're being welcomed back into your own family home. Often the women of the family spend hours, even days, in the kitchen preparing mezze that can cover entire tables.

If you don't like lemon, garlic or olive oil, Lebanon may not be the place for you. But if you're like me and love this magical combination, you're in for a treat as it forms the basis for dips, marinades, salad dressings and much more. Some of my favourite Lebanese barbecue foods include kofta (ground meat and parsley), hummus (chickpea dip), vine leaves (vine leaves around rice and/or meat), tabouleh (parsley, tomato and cracked wheat salad), citrus marinades, dips, olives, cheese and nuts. These are often enjoyed along with beer, wine or Arak, the national alcoholic aniseed-flavoured drink of Lebanon.

LEBANESE TABOULI

TRADITIONALLY A VERY FINE CRACKED wheat is used for this dish which does not need to be soaked beforehand as the juice from the tomatoes and the oil and lemon juice plump up the grains while it sits for hours in the fridge. However, coarser cracked wheat seems to be more readily available, so in this recipe the grains are soaked.

Put the tabouli in a serving dish and cover with water. Leave for about 40 minutes (while you prepare everything else) or until the grains have plumped up. Drain well and put into a large bowl. Put the tomatoes on top (without stirring), then the parsley and spring onions. Drizzle over the oil and lemon juice and season well with salt and black pepper, again do not stir. Put into the fridge for at least 2 hours to allow the flavours to mingle and the grains to soak up the juice.

Remove from the fridge 20 minutes before serving. Just before serving, mix everything together well and transfer to a serving dish.

PREP: 45 minutes
SERVES: 6-8

80g (½ cup) tabouli (crushed wheat)
4 tomatoes, finely chopped
2 bunches (about 220g) curly parsley, leaves only, finely chopped
1 bunch of spring onions, finely chopped
160ml (2/3 cup) good quality olive oil
80ml (1/3 cup) lemon juice
Salt and freshly ground black pepper

LEBANESE GARLIC CHICKEN

TO MAKE THE MARINADE/SAUCE it's easiest if you have a small food processor, alternatively use a bowl and whisk. Put the garlic and salt in a food processor (or bowl) and mash to a smoothish paste. With the engine running or with whisk at the ready, very gradually add the olive oil and then the lemon juice until you have a smooth consistency. (If you add the oil too fast you will end up with garlic sitting in oil, rather than a sauce consistency.) Reserve about 2 tablespoons of the marinade for serving with the cooked chicken. Put the chicken into a ziplock bag, add the remaining marinade and rub all over the chicken for a few minutes. Put in the fridge to marinate for at least 2 hours and up to 24.

Remove the chicken for the fridge 20 minutes before grilling to return to room temperature. Preheat barbecue to medium. Different pieces of meat will require different cooking times. Turn the chicken fairly regularly to ensure even cooking. The skin can blacken a bit but don't let it burn too much. Ensure the chicken is cooked through before serving. Cook wings for about 20 minutes, legs and thighs for 15-20 minutes and breast for 10-12 minutes.

PREP: 15 minutes
COOK: about 20 minutes
SERVES: 4-6

6 garlic cloves, crushed
½ teaspoon salt
100ml olive oil
2 tablespoons lemon juice
6 pieces of chicken: leg, thigh or breast (preferably skin on)

KOFTA

FOR A REALLY AUTHENTIC MEAL, serve these delicious, meaty kofta with hummus and a tomato and onion salad. They can be prepared in advance and cooked just before serving. The mixture can easily be halved and if you want smaller entree sized ones, just make them half the size and cook them for less time.

If using wooden skewers, soak them in cold water for 20 minutes to prevent them from burning.

Put all the kofta ingredients, except the meat and egg into a food processor and process into a smooth paste. Transfer to a bowl, add the mince and egg and using your hands mix thoroughly until smooth. (If you don't have a food processor, chop everything finely and mix well.) Divide the mixture into 12 (or 24 if making smaller ones) and mould into sausage shapes around the skewers.

Preheat barbecue to medium-hot. It is preferable to keep the meat away from direct heat, so if possible put 2 bricks on the barbecue a kebab-skewer-length apart. Rest the kebabs on the bricks and cook, turning a couple of times for 15-20 minutes, or until browned and cooked through. If cooking the kebabs directly on the barbecue they will cook more quickly. Quickly toast the pitta breads and split open. Delicious served with hummus and salad.

PREP: 40 minutes
COOK: 15-20 minutes
MAKES: 12 big kofta or 24 small ones

1½ bunches parsley, leaves only, roughly chopped
1 bunch mint, leaves only, roughly chopped
4 spring onions, chopped
1 teaspoon salt
Freshly ground black pepper
1 medium-hot red chilli, seeded and chopped
¼ teaspoon ground cumin
¼ teaspoon ground coriander
½ teaspoon harissa (optional)
1kg beef or lamb mince
1 egg, lightly beaten

TO SERVE:
Whole wheat pitta bread
Tomato & onion salad (from Turkish lamb kebabs, p 68,) optional
Hummus (p 133), optional

RAMADAN

In Egypt, there are no half measures. There is the Sahara Desert, the great Sphinx and pyramids of Giza, alongside the arguably world's longest river, the Nile. And when it comes to feasts, it won't be outdone. Like other Islamic areas, during the holy month of Ramadan there is fasting from dawn to dusk. This is followed by a three-day feast when lambs or other animals are sacrificed and barbecued, before being shared with family, friends and the less fortunate.

It's this last part that emphasises the kind and giving nature of people around a barbecue. We should all keep this in mind next time we over-cater at a barbecue – offer to share your delights with people less fortunate, as barbecuing is meant to be enjoyed by all.

THE FIVE SENSES OF A MIDDLE EASTERN BARBECUE

A Middle Eastern barbecue is sure to create a lasting memory for all the senses. Tony, our gracious host, explained: 'The importance of mezze can't be overlooked. The bite-sized mezze brings your taste buds to life and allows time to socialise and interact with family and friends without distraction before the main meal'. Mezze dishes are often eaten with your hands as your sense of touch is called upon by the never ending breads, olives, meats and dips passing through your fingers.

Then, as the barbecue continues and the main meal is enjoyed, the sights and sounds of unmistakable Middle Eastern music, dancing and singing take over. If you're lucky enough you may also see some traditional belly dancing.

At the end of the meal it's time for your sense of smell to be awakened. Strong and thick Arabic coffee mixed with the aroma of sweet apple- and fruit-scented tobacco smoke fills the air as hookahs (or Lebanese 'argileh') are passed around. It's a true five-senses experience.

ISRAELI SALADS

ISRAELI SALADS

At an Israeli barbecue the salads are the most important part of the meal. Most barbecues will feature a minimum of six or seven salads, always including hummus and tahina and usually a spicy tomato salad. Pitta bread is also a must and the salads are crammed into the pitta along with some meat.

These recipes serve 6 if served as part of a selection of salads, otherwise they serve 3 or 4. Each salad can be prepared in less than 20 minutes.

DILL SALAD WITH MAYONNAISE

2-3 tablespoons finely chopped fresh dill
Salt and freshly ground black pepper
8 gherkins (dill pickles) (about 175g), cut into 1cm cubes
125g small can corn kernels, drained
1 red capsicum, diced
3 tablespoons mayonnaise.

Soak the dill in salted water for 5 minutes. Drain well then put in a bowl with the gherkins, corn and red capsicum. Mix well. Add the mayonnaise, season with salt and pepper and mix gently. Chill then serve.

SERIOUSLY GARLICKY CARROT SALAD

1 juicy lemon (roll it on the counter a few times to make it even juicier)
3 medium (about 550g) carrots, grated
4-5 garlic cloves, finely chopped
Big pinch of salt

Finely grate one teaspoon of zest from the lemon and squeeze the juice from the lemon. Put the carrots and garlic in a bowl, add the lemon juice and zest and some salt. Mix well and set aside to allow the flavours to develop.

TOMATO AND CHILLI SALAD

6 firm, ripe tomatoes
4 garlic cloves, finely chopped
2 small red chillies, seeded and finely chopped
1 tablespoon oil

1 teaspoon salt

Cut a cross into the base of each tomato. Put into a bowl of boiling water for 5-10 seconds then plunge into a bowl of cold water. Peel the tomatoes then dice. Put into a bowl then add the garlic, chilli, oil and salt. Combine and set aside to allow the flavours to develop.

SPICY SPRING (GREEN) ONION SALAD

1 bunch spring (green) onions, sliced
4-6 radishes, chopped
1 red chilli, finely chopped
1 large red capsicum, cubed
1 bunch parsley, roughly chopped
Juice of 1 lemon
1 tablespoon olive oil
Salt and freshly ground black pepper.

Put all the vegetables and the parsley in a serving dish and mix. Drizzle over the lemon juice and oil, season with salt and black pepper and toss everything together. Set aside to allow the flavours to mingle.

MARINATED EGGPLANT SALAD

2 gherkins (dill pickles), diced
1 red capsicum, cubed
3 French shallots (or half an onion), roughly chopped
1 small bunch flat-leaf parsley, roughly chopped
Juice of 1 lemon
Salt
1 tablespoon olive oil, plus extra for shallow frying
450-500g small eggplant, sliced into 1 cm circles

Combine the gherkins, capsicum, shallots and parsley in a bowl. Add the lemon juice, a little salt and 1 tablespoon olive oil. Mix well and set aside for at least 30 minutes before serving.

Heat 2-3 tablespoons of olive oil in a shallow frying pan over medium heat. Fry the eggplant slices in a single layer (you will have to do this in batches).

and for about 5-6 minutes turning once, until golden. Cool on kitchen paper.

Arrange the eggplant slices in a couple of layers in a shallow serving dish. Pour over the marinade and serve.

A lean dinner

Perfection in the making

CHERMOULA FISH

CHERMOULA IS A CLASSIC MOROCCAN marinade, used predominantly for fish. If you want to make kebabs instead of serving whole pieces of fish, just cut the fish into cubes before marinating. Thread onto skewers before grilling. You can also use the marinade on whole fish. Put some inside the fish as well.

Combine all the ingredients except the fish. Put the fish in a shallow dish and pour over the marinade. Turn to coat the fish and leave to marinate for at least an hour and up to 12 hours.

Preheat barbecue to hot. Remove the fish from the marinade, reserving the marinade. Cook the fish for 8-10 minutes, turning once, or until cooked through. The cooking time will depend on the thickness of your fish. Brush some of the reserved chermoula on the fish during the first half of cooking. If cooking kebabs, turn and baste regularly while cooking.

Serve the fish accompanied by salad and potatoes.

PREP: 14 minutes
COOK: 8-10 minutes
MAKES: 4-6 servings

3 tablespoons chopped fresh coriander leaves
3 tablespoons chopped fresh flat-leaf parsley
2 garlic cloves, crushed
1 teaspoon ground cumin
1 teaspoon ground coriander
2 teaspoons paprika
3 tablespoons lemon juice (1-1½ lemons)
125ml (½ cup) olive oil
4-6 firm fish fillets

Must have heard there was a barbecue!

Spices aren't from a jar?

EGYPTIAN SALAD

PUT THE GARLIC INTO THE OIL AND set aside so the garlic can flavour the oil.

Put the tomatoes, chillies, red onion, chickpeas, coriander and mint leaves in a serving bowl and mix gently. Scatter over the feta. Drizzle over the oil (without the garlic) and squeeze over the lemon juice. Serve.

PREP: 20 minutes
SERVES: 4

1 garlic clove, squashed (not crushed)
3 tablespoons olive oil
3-4 (about 250g) firm, ripe tomatoes, chopped
2 small green chillies, seeded and sliced
1 small red onion, chopped
400g can chickpeas, drained, rinsed and drained well again
Small handful coriander leaves
Small handful mint leaves
100g feta, finely crumbled
½ a lemon

SHEEP CUTS

Like the cow, the meat that comes from the top of the sheep is the most tender. Cutlets are quick and fast and a rack of lamb looks pretty impressive. For kebabs go for cuts like neck and leg fillet. For a quick but spectacular barbecue offering get your butcher to butterfly a leg of lamb. It's happy to be left alone on the barbie while you have a beer, and there's no bone to worry about when carving.

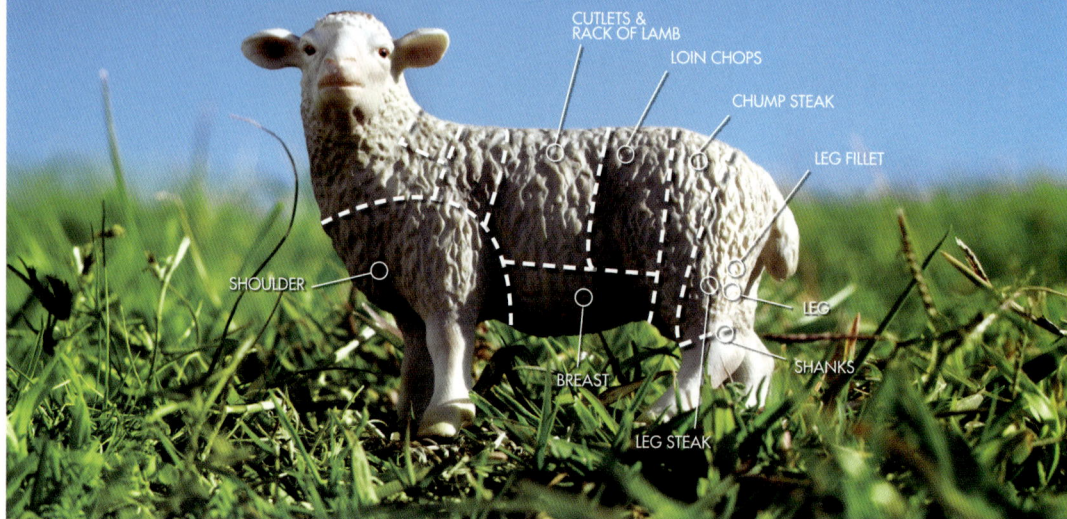

CUTLETS & RACK OF LAMB
LOIN CHOPS
CHUMP STEAK
LEG FILLET
SHOULDER
LEG
SHANKS
BREAST
LEG STEAK

ORANGES AND POMEGRANATE IN ROSEWATER SUGAR SYRUP

THIS CAN EASILY BE PREPARED IN advance. Keep the three components separate and assemble just before serving.

Put 250ml (1 cup) water and the sugar in a small saucepan over medium heat and stir until the sugar dissolves, without boiling. Once the sugar has dissolved, add the orange juice, bring to the boil and simmer for 5 minutes. Add the rose syrup and simmer for 1 minute more. Leave to cool then strain through a sieve. Chill.

Meanwhile, using a sharp knife slice the top and bottom off each orange to give a stable base, then carefully slice off the skin and pith, slicing from top to bottom. Slice each orange into rounds about 1cm (½ in) thick. Arrange on a serving platter, preferably one with a lip. Scatter over the pomegranate seeds and pour over the rose syrup. Serve.

PREP: 30 minutes
COOK: about 8 minutes
MAKES: 6 servings

110g (1/2 cup) caster sugar
80ml (1/3 cup) fresh orange juice (about 1 orange)
3 teaspoons rose water
1 medium pomegranate, seeds only, pith discarded
4 oranges

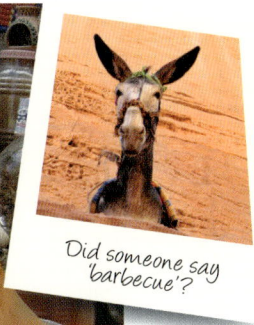

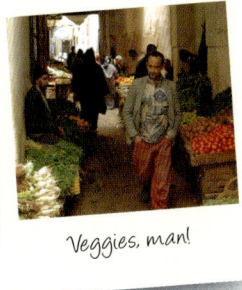

Did someone say 'barbecue'?

Veggies, man!

WHERE THERE'S SMOKE, THERE'S FIRE
A GUIDE TO BBQ SAFETY

THESE POINTS ARE A BEGINNER'S GUIDE to barbecue safety and do not replace the official manufacturer's rules, regulations and guidelines for barbecue use and safety.

It is important that you always refer to the instruction manuals, warranties and safety guides provided by the manufacturer as these are written with particular barbecues in mind and may vary between manufacturers and countries.

- Most important – always read the safety instructions. Each new barbecue should include a set of instructions outlining important procedures to ensure safe preparation and ongoing use of your barbecue. If these are not included, contact the manufacturer or the place of purchase.

■ Most obvious – gas in flammable! It may seem strange to many of you that I am pointing this out, but in the excitement that accompanies a new barbecue many people forget the danger. Remember, the longer you leave the gas running before lighting, the bigger the flame. If the barbecue doesn't light at first go, turn it off and wait at least 45 seconds for the unused gas to clear before trying again.

■ Initial set-up – ensure all fittings are securely tightened, gas burners are correctly sitting over the gas cocks and there are no gas leaks. To check this prior to use, brush soapy water over all connections; if you see bubbles, re-tighten and test again. Regularly check the hose and regulator for cracks and leaks. If in doubt, throw them out. Gas barbecues are not to be used indoors. Real Men Do it Outdoors!

■ Charcoal barbecues – the more fuel you use, the more fire and heat it will create. Make sure the barbecue is positioned away from anything else that may catch fire or be affected by the heat.

■ Gas cylinders – these are to be treated like a glass of beer. Always ensure they remain upright and out of direct sunlight. When the cylinder gets too old, get it checked or get a new one – refer to manufacturer guidelines regarding frequency. There should be a stamp on the side of the bottle indicating the date when the bottle was last tested, but if in doubt contact your gas supplier for advice. Also do not light a cigarette or fires close to the cylinder and remember to turn the gas cylinder off in between each use of the barbecue.

■ Fat/oil – always keep the drip tray full of a fat-absorbing substance, or empty old oil build-ups to prevent fat fires from occurring. You may find this type of fire is not covered by warranties, so don't cut corners.

■ Indoor use – barbecues are not designed to be used indoors. If it rains, build a pergola, or order a pizza.

■ If you don't know exactly what you are doing, especially with regulators, hoses and gas leaks, don't try to be a 'mister fix-it'. Use official parts and consult professionals; $15 for a new part is cheaper than the burns unit.

No more lectures. Sit back, relax, crack a coldie and get on with the barbie.

ANATOMY OF A BBQ – A GUIDE TO ALL THOSE UNKNOWN PARTS

1. Frame – steel frame covered in paint or vitreous enamel.
2. Trolley – holds BBQ up; often metal and/or timber.
3. Roasting Hood – turns BBQ into roasting oven.
4. Rain Lid – protects cooking surface from the weather; not for roasting.
5. Hose & Regulator – left hand thread; regulates gas flow; connects BBQ to cylinder.
6. Gas Cylinder/Bottle – fuel source; turn off between use (turn burners off first).
7. Plates and Grills – generally cast iron or steel; always keep well oiled.
8. Burners – source of heat. Cast iron or metal; sit over gas cocks.
9. Drip Tray – catches fat from food; always fill with recommended fat-absorbing material to prevent fat fires.
10. Rock Tray – distributes heat evenly under grill; requires lava/ceramic rock.
11. Flame Tamers/Diverters – distributes heat evenly under grill; does not require lava/ceramic rock.
12. Lava/Ceramic Rock – sits on top of rock tray, replace regularly.
13. Auto Ignition – built-in ignition system for your BBQ.
14. Gas Cocks – feeds gas from manifold to burners.
15. Side Burner – for wok cooking.
16. Manifold – supplies gas to burners.

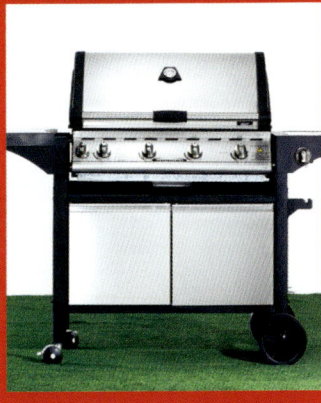

SCRUBBERS GUIDE TO MINIMAL
CLEANING AND MAINTENANCE

POSSIBLY THE GREATEST advantage of outdoor cooking over conventional indoor kitchens is the minimal amount of effort required to keep the barbecue clean.

The following is a guide only – always refer to your specific barbecue instructions to ensure you are treating your barbecue correctly.

COOKING SURFACE
The one golden rule for maintaining the perfect cooking surface is 'You can never use too much cooking oil'. After cooking, scrape off any excess food and grime and apply an extra coating of oil to the plate to protect it between uses. An easy way to do this is with a cooking spray.

After the barbecue has cooled down, remember to replace the rain lid or cooking hood to protect the cooking surface from the elements. Before re-using, heat the barbecue and repeat the process.

BARBECUE FRAME AND ROASTING HOOD
If your barbecue looks as though it has reached the point of no return or you are looking for an effort-free alternative, you'll find barbie clean-ing sprays at all major retailers. They are a little like oven cleaners for the barbecue.

TROLLEYS
There has been a shift towards all metal trolleys as they require much less maintenance than hardwood trolleys which should be treated regularly with natural oil to prevent the wood from drying, fading and cracking. Also, due to hardwood expanding or contracting as the weather changes, the bolts holding the trolley together will need tightening from time to time. Metal trolleys, on the other hand, only require scratches to be touched up with a standard metal paint to avoid rust.

DRIP TRAY
The drip tray will need to be cleaned out regularly and, if needed, refilled with a fat-absorbing substance available from barbecue stores, every 3-6 months depending upon frequency of use. Because many barbecues are not covered against fat fires, it is recommended that a proper absorbent product be used. If you don't have any on hand, then sand is a good short-term solution.

ROCK TRAY/ FLAME TAMERS
For gas barbecues, flame tamers and ceramic rocks are now a more convenient option than lava rock, which was a popular choice for many years, but needed to be replaced every 6-12 months depending on frequency of use. If you still have lava rock, it is generally time to replace the rocks when they can no longer absorb any more fat and are starting to catch fire and remain on fire.

CHARCOAL AND WOODBARBECUES
Clean out old ash and check that all air vents and moving parts are well lubricated and moving as intended, to ensure everything is working properly prior to use.

GAS BURNERS
A light layer of cooking oil can be applied to the burners to help prevent rust; however, due to constant heat this will not have a lasting effect. A wire brush can also be used to clean the burners and prolong their life. Rotate them regularly and protect them from wear and tear is the best advice.

HOSE AND REGULATORS
Keep these free of knots and kinks. It is also important to keep a close eye on these for cracks and fraying. If in doubt, replace immediately.

IN SUMMARY
So that you and your barbecue share a long, trouble-free life together, keep it sheltered from the weather, pay attention to the condition of all parts and fittings and replace immediately if in doubt. Don't be afraid to use lots of cooking oil.

THYME

SEA SALT

CAJUN

PIRI PIRI

TARRAGON

SAGE

FENNEL SEEDS

BARBECUE SMOKEY
SEASONING

CHINESE FIVE SPICE

CORIANDER

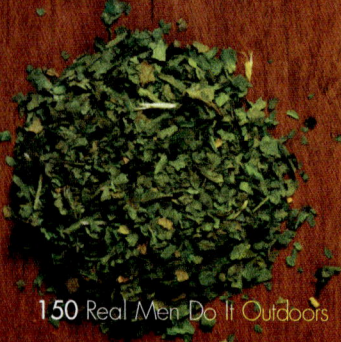

ROSEMARY

PAPRIKA

CORIANDER

MINT

HERBS & SPICES

Buy fresh herbs either in pots or in bunches. If you buy bunches keep them fresh by wrapping them in damp kitchen paper, then store in a plastic bag in the salad crisper of your fridge. You'll get the most flavour from the herbs when they are either bruised or chopped, as this releases the essential oils.

BASIL

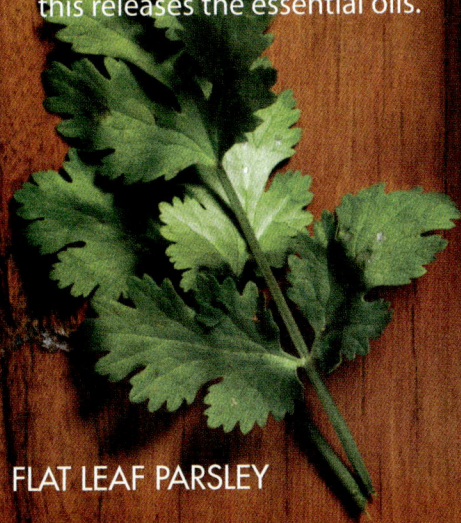

FLAT LEAF PARSLEY

THYME

PARSLEY – We have used Flat-leaf (also called Italian) parsley in our recipes. Use it in marinades and sauces or use loads of the leaves in salads for added flavour.

MINT – Mint goes very well with potatoes so is delicious in potato salad. It's also ideal in Middle Eastern-style marinades and sauces or just add a handful to an Asian noodle salad.

BASIL – Where would a tomato salad be without basil? A delicious herb that just shouts summer. Chop some up and add to mayonnaise, add a little to French dressing or scatter a handful over sliced tomatoes with a drizzle of good olive oil and a dash of balsamic vinegar.

THYME – Thyme is a more woody herb, but its leaves are soft. It has quite a strong flavour but is great in marinades. For a speedy way to add flavour, dip a small bunch of thyme into seasoned olive oil and use as a basting brush for meat and fish while cooking.

CORIANDER – One of those herbs that you love or hate! For the lovers amongst us, chop up and add to marinades for fish, chicken or pork. Its intense aromatic flavour also goes very well with chilli.

DRIED HERBS AND SPICES – It's useful to keep a few jars of herbs and spices in your cupboard for adding instant flavour. When using dried herbs use in small quantities as they have an intense flavour. However, they don't really keep for more than 6 months before they start to lose their flavour, so buy in small quantities.

THYME – Dried thyme is one of the more useful dried herbs to keep in your cupboard. Use sparingly in marinades or in rubs. It's particularly good with chicken and fish.

SEA SALT – It's generally not a good idea to salt meat before you cook it on the barbie as this can draw out the delicious juices. Salt the meat after it is cooked. Sea and rock salt are delicious scattered over root vegetables when baking.

CAJUN – A mixture of spices ideal for flavouring fish, chicken, meat and prawns. Usually contains paprika, cayenne, garlic, oregano, thyme, salt and pepper. It is not necessarily fiery hot.

PIRI PIRI – This is a very spicy, small chilli pepper which can be bought ground, flaked or as a sauce. Good in spice rubs, marinades and bastes. A handy spice to keep in your cupboard.

TARRAGON – Unfortunately, this often bears little resemblance to fresh tarragon and loses its flavour quickly, so buy in small quantities. Use in rubs or sauces.

GROUND CORIANDER – With quite a different taste to the fresh leaves this is the ground up seeds of the coriander plant. Used widely in Middle Eastern-style cooking. Mix with some olive oil and rub over lamb chops before barbecing.

FENNEL SEEDS – These have an aniseed-liquorice flavour and taste slightly sweet. Good for rubbing onto the skin of oily fish before barbecuing or try rubbing some into pork chops or pork loin.

BARBECUE SMOKY SEASONING – This is a good mixture to buy if you don't want to have a wide variety of spices in your cupboard. Use either as a rub on its own or combine with olive oil and brush over meat or fish as it cooks to add both flavour and moisture.

CHINESE FIVE SPICE – This is an easy-to-find blend of spices, consisting of equal parts Sichuan pepper, cassis or cinnamon, fennel seeds, star anise and cloves. Particularly good with beef and pork.

DRIED CORIANDER – Dried coriander is the ground up seeds of the coriander plant. It's useful in marinades and fantastic when you want a North African or Asian flavour. Don't keep it too long otherwise it will just end up taking like musty dust!

DRIED ROSEMARY – This is a strongly flavoured herb, so use sparingly. Good with sausages and pork.

PAPRIKA – Paprika can range in flavour from mild to hot, so use sparingly if you're not sure how hot yours is, although it should say somewhere on the label. Combine with a little olive oil and brush over meat before and during barbecuing. Serve with a little lemon squeezed over.

RECIPE INDEX BY BEER RATING

INDEX BY REGION & RECIPE

ACKNOWLEDGMENTS

My most sincere thanks must go to Katy Holder, my fantastic food editor, recipe writer and food stylist on both this book and the previous one **Real Men Do it Outdoors**. Katy has taken the reams of ideas, scribbled recipes and notes created from my wanderings around the world and turned them into the easy, achievable recipes that appear in this book.

I am also indebted to Katy, Jon, Wendy and Joey for the delicious looking food shots.

With thanks to MUD Australia for the loan of props.

With thanks to Claudia Hernandez and Galit Oren for additional advice on Mexican and Israeli recipes and the loan of props.

With thanks to Barbeques Galore and my friends at the Moore Park store for all their help & advice.

To my wife Laura for all her support and patience during the long and challenging development of both **Real Men** books.

To the handsome Barbie 'lifestyle models' (ha!), Trav, Playboy, Doogs & Daniel. To my great friends (Trav & Mel, Adam & Hayley, Grant & Janet (Granet) & Scotty (Doogs)) who contributed photos. Robert Owens, for many great US Barbie pics and to Charlie & Illya Shackell for the photos of Asian markets. And thanks to Peta Xanthoudakis of 'Location Shots' for her barbecue photoshoot.

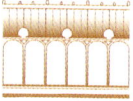

LONGUEVILLE
MEDIA

Published in 2010 by
Longueville Media Pty Ltd
PO Box 102 Double Bay
New South Wales 1360 Australia

www.longmedia.com.au
info@longmedia.com.au
T. 02 9362 8441

Food Stylist/Editor: Katy Holder
Home Economist: Wendy Quisumbing
Photographer: Jon Bader
Photographer's assistant: Joey Molines
Interior design: Justin Golby

Cataloguing in Publication
Barnes, Joshua, 1978- .
Real men do it outdoors around the world : the bloke's BBQ cookbook /Joshua Barnes.
ISBN: 9781920681623 (pbk.)
Barbecue cooking, Cooking.
641.5784